Planning for Success

Planning for Success

A practical guide to setting and achieving
your social media marketing goals

Luan Wise

ISBNs
Paperback 978 1 7394578 0 8
E-book 978 1 7394578 1 5

Praise for:

Planning for Success:
A practical guide to setting and achieving
your social media marketing goals

Some people can make the simple appear complex and others who are truly gifted in their profession can make the complex, simple. Luan Wise has the ability to retain all of the sophistication of social media marketing and present it without needing to make it complex. *Planning for Success* is a valuable read for business and students alike – social media marketing made simply sophisticated!
Professor Jonathan Deacon, University of South Wales.

Many of us love scrolling social media; some of us even post content for others. Using social media for commercial benefit though is tough. *Planning for Success* takes a difficult challenge and breaks it into bite-size chunks. If you want to use social media strategically, this is the first book you should read.
Dr Thomas Bowden Green, University of the West of England.

As someone who has often experienced imposter syndrome in the world of social media, *Planning for Success* offered me a much-needed sense of assurance. Learning from an expert like Luan Wise, who has a wealth of experience in the field, felt like a personalised mentorship that has immensely contributed to my professional growth. I found this book to be an enlightening and empowering resource.
Tinisha Osu, Early career marketer. BSc Psychology and Biology. MSc Forensic Psychology.

This book is for everyone who would like to gain an understanding in the ever-changing field of social media. *Planning for Success* takes you on the complete social media marketing journey, stripping back the complex topic to allow you not just to understand all the various aspects, but also how to utilise them to achieve your goals, and measure the results. It's the perfect no-nonsense guide.
Anna Miller, Early career marketer. BA (Hons) Marketing.

Planning for Success is packed full of golden nuggets. Working in social media is fast-paced so it's great to have a book that you can dip back in to as a reminder of the fundamentals you need for planning and creating campaigns. However you get to engage with Luan, whether it's through reading her books, consultancy, training or events, you'll feel more confident and inspired. I love that I've had the opportunity to work with Luan and now I've got all her great advice written down in one handy reference guide!
Elizabeth Starling, Social Media Manager.

Planning for Success is an educational read for anyone working in social media marketing. Luan comprehensively and knowledgeably talks you through a process for building a solid social media plan designed to support the overall business strategy. Luan's step-by-step approach to it all explains both the 'why' and 'how', including brilliant case study examples across different industries and sectors, useful template resources and directions for onward research and learning if required. Too often social media is dumbed down and disregarded, yet so much can be achieved with its strategic use. Reading this book will help you develop the knowledge to do so!
Beth Kirk, Social Media Marketing Coach.

Once I started reading, I couldn't put it down. This book is an essential guide if you're using social media to market your organisation. Whether, like me, you've worked in social media for a decade, or you're just starting out, there is a lesson for everyone. Why? Because this book uses data from industry professionals, case studies and expert opinions to provide you with best practices. This book will blow your mind, enable you to build smart strategies and send you on the path to social media success. I love this book, an absolute 10/10.
Jake Potter, Head of Social Media.

Planning for Success by Luan Wise is a must-read for anyone in social media or any other kind of marketing. The insights are clear and actionable, turning complex ideas into straightforward steps. This book is a practical guide for setting and achieving marketing goals. I'm going to go so far as to say it's the best book on the realities of planning social media that I have read.
Claire Hattrick, FCIM. Associate Director, Marketing.

I've had the benefit of knowing Luan for nearly a decade. She has probably forgotten more about social media marketing than I know. Fortunately for me, and you, she's distilled a significant chunk of it down into *Planning for Success.* It's an excellent book with supporting online tools that will get you excited about levelling up your social media marketing at a time when many professionals are probably feeling fatigued by it all. With its comprehensive and chronological work-a-long style, it's going to help you rapidly apply sound, strategic principles to practical implementation. Don't waste a minute, grab your copy and start putting Luan's model to work today!
René Power, B2B Marketing Consultant.

Contents

- Understanding change in social media
- An introduction to LinkedIn, Twitter, Facebook, Instagram,
  TikTok and Snapchat
- A note about YouTube
- Case study: Xero, Serial Killer Receipts
- The marketing funnel
- Chapter summary
- Actions

- Strategy vs tactics
- Finding your purpose
- Setting objectives
- Case study: The use of LinkedIn by Cheltenham Borough
  Council
- Chapter summary
- Actions

- Digital natives and digital immigrants
- Challenging assumptions and stereotypes

- A clear vision of your products and services
- Market segmentation
- Case study: Hilton
- Selecting your target market
- The key stakeholders behind a buying decision
- Customer personas
- Chapter summary
- Actions

Chapter 4: Examining the social media competition

- Types of competitor
- Analysing competitors' social media presence
- Your competitors' advertising activity
- Social media listening
- Case study: ContentCal. Leveraging competitor listening for business growth
- How to choose the right social media platforms for your organisation
- Case study: Using social media to gather insights
- Chapter summary
- Actions

Chapter 5: Creating a social media content calendar

- Personal branding and thought leadership
- Case study: Involving subject matter experts in content creation
- Ideas before format
- A note about organic and paid social media
- The importance of storytelling
- Case study: Airbnb's storytelling through social media
- What are content pillars?
- Establishing your content pillars
- Creating a content calendar
- Evergreen content
- Repurposing content

List of figures

Foreword

By Professor Laura Chamberlain
Professor of Marketing, Warwick Business School, The University of Warwick.

It is genuinely a pleasure when someone in your professional sphere becomes a friend. Luan and I got to know each other through our mutual love of marketing, and it is always a pleasure to work with her as her passion for learning matches my own. We are regularly to be found having wide-ranging and enriching conversations about all aspects of marketing and I particularly enjoy her wit, insight and ability to question the norm.

Luan describes herself as a T-shaped marketer and her expertise is outstanding. What is particularly noteworthy about this book is its accessibility. Luan's friendly sunny nature shines through her writing, she explains concepts and frameworks clearly and articulately without using intimidating language or acronyms. Whether you are a student, someone new to social media, or a seasoned social media professional, this book is for you.

I describe this as the book that keeps on giving. There are of course key principles, but also actions, examples, practical advice and a framework to help navigate social media, to apply learning and empower readers to design their own best course of action. Luan works on the principle that a cookie-cutter 'how to' guide isn't appropriate in a fast-changing landscape and that's precisely why this book adds so much value and will be useful to so many people. This book allows you to find the optimal strategy for you, your objectives and your business.

From my perspective as a marketing educator, the underpinning theme of strategy is the bedrock of success and Luan brilliantly explains how to approach this, and importantly, how tactics should feed from strategy and not the other way around. Social media is not just a job to give an intern or something people can do alongside an already full workload. It is important as a marketing activity and it is hugely valuable when executed well. This book will enable social media success and presents a good mix of theory and practice to facilitate this.

At the outset of this project, Luan knew she wanted robust and unique insights to shape her work which is why this book also presents research that we conducted to help to explore and explain what we see happening in the world of social media marketing. Luan has always said it is important to find out what's really going on and we decided to do things a little differently and use our combined expertise to really dig into issues.

I am wholeheartedly recommending this book to my marketing friends, my students, graduates and fellow marketing educators. A wide range of topics are covered from the marketing funnel to purpose, and how to create content pillars and a content calendar. Luan mixes real-life examples from her vast professional experience and has unique insights from a range of leading experts. This is the perfect book for someone starting out in the world of social media, or for a seasoned professional to dip in and out of as all the essentials are in one place. It is easy to get bogged down in the day-to-day and lose sight of core principles, so this will have pride of place on my desk to help me every day. I know Luan will appreciate that I want to dive in with my highlighter and start making notes in the margin of my copy already! I am already finding this useful and I am so glad that Luan has shared her wisdom with you too. Enjoy!

Introduction

Welcome to my book, *Planning for Success: A practical guide to setting and achieving your social media marketing goals*.

In November 2016 I self-published the book *Relax! It's Only Social Media*, which went on to win a National Indie Excellence Award. This book was intended to be a second edition, to bring the text up to date. Little did I know that what I initially envisioned as simple changes would turn into an entirely new book.

I started planning this book in 2019, with the idea of publishing it in 2020. Well, I don't think anything went to plan during the unprecedented global pandemic. I think, and hope, that the delay has made this book better and more relevant than ever.

Relax! now represents a collection of my knowledge from 2016, while *Planning for Success* embodies everything I have learned since then, through working with clients, conducting training courses, and immersing myself in reading and observation.

I also asked for reader feedback and am hugely grateful to those that got involved in focus groups to discuss the first book and requirements for a second. I hope I've responded to every one of the requests!

One reviewer quote that resonated with me profoundly and influenced the direction of this book was 'This is the book my students need before they go into industry.'

Planning for Success is for early career marketers, digital natives entering the workforce, and digital immigrants who are navigating their way through the ever-changing world of social media.

I strongly believe that planning is the cornerstone of success. All too often, individuals dive into social media, hastily setting up profiles and creating posts without planning out what they want to achieve. This needs to stop. The perception that social media marketing is a role for interns needs to change. Senior marketers and business leaders need to pay attention to this media channel, which continues to grow. There is no 'right' or 'wrong', but there are good and poor practices.

I understand the challenges of writing a book about a topic that changes daily. This is not a 'how to' guide. I can't tell you exactly what to do, but I can hopefully show you an approach and help you find answers to your questions. I have tried to provide a framework that will remain relevant, regardless of the dynamic nature of the social media landscape.

You will likely take a 'holiday read' approach and read the book through quickly, in its entirety, and then return to each chapter.

At the end of each chapter, you will find a list of recommended actions. These are all summarised again at the end of the book. The intention is that you will be able to build a one-page social media marketing plan as you follow each chapter.

Throughout the book, I have used the term 'organisation'. I believe the content of the book is as applicable to commercial businesses, as it is to not-for-profit and educational institutions.

I hope that as you read the book you will come to understand how important it is to align social media with your business plan, to set appropriate social media objectives, and to plan content that will engage your target audience. I also hope that you will feel more confident about measuring what matters – and that you are prepared for any issues that might arise.

Don't forget to follow and connect with me on social media: @luanwise.

Let's get started...

A research-led approach

The content of this book is underpinned by a research project conducted in collaboration with Warwick Business School, University of Warwick.

I first met Laura when an undergraduate marketing student invited me to speak to their marketing society about LinkedIn. From the moment we crossed paths, I've welcomed every opportunity to spend time with Laura, sharing thoughts, ideas and asking questions.

Over a coffee, I updated Laura on my thinking for a second version of my book, *Relax! It's Only Social Media*, and how I wanted to explore some of my client and training conversations in more depth. We opened our laptops and started to scope an idea to examine the use of social media in small and medium-sized organisations (SMEs).

The research proposal received approval from the University of Warwick Humanities & Social Sciences Research Ethics Committee in March 2020. We debated whether to proceed with the research at this time (as the world was heading into lockdown), but with our glasses half-full decided we should continue. Now, we appreciate our opportunity to obtain insights into the use of social media at such a pivotal time in our history.

By May 2020, 238 marketers had provided anonymous responses to our online questionnaire. Participants were recruited using personal networks and via the research software company Qualtrics. The following criteria applied: aged over 18 and working in marketing at a UK-based organisation with up to 250 employees.

We also conducted ten qualitative interviews. For these, participants were recruited using personal networks. Thus, most interviewees were already known to the interviewers. Interviews were conducted using video-conferencing software and lasted for approx. twenty minutes. Participation was voluntary, and no incentives were provided. Any information obtained during the interviews remains confidential and any details used have been anonymised.

In November 2022 we repeated the survey, using the same collection approach and criteria: 178 marketers provided anonymous responses to the online questionnaire, and ten qualitative interviews were undertaken.

Between May 2020 and November 2022, five organisations completed surveys before social media training. These were completed by both marketers and non-marketers, and any details used have been anonymised.

Not all the research findings are included in the book: however, the review of academic literature to prepare the survey, and the responses from both the online questionnaires and qualitative interviews, have informed and shaped the content significantly. Although research-led, the book is not solely a presentation of a research study; it draws from a diverse array of sources, including real-life experiences.

If you would like further details about the research, please email sayhello@luanwise.co.uk

The one-page social media marketing plan

This book intends to help you create a one-page social media marketing plan. The plan will become your reference for everything you do, from content creation to posting and measurement.

The template is shown below, along with an indication of the chapter where you will find the information. At the end of each chapter is a list of actions, and these are also summarised at the end of the book.

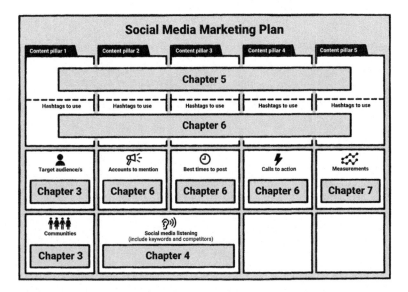

The template can be accessed (for free) by visiting my website at www.luanwise.co.uk/books/planning-for-success/one-page-plan or by scanning the QR code below.

Alongside the one-page plan, the book will also guide you to prepare and use:

- Customer personas (Chapter 3)
- Competitor insight reports (Chapter 4)
- Content calendars (Chapter 5)
- A content inventory (Chapter 5)
- Brand and tone of voice guidelines (Chapter 6)
- Reporting templates (Chapter 7)
- A social media policy (Chapter 8)
- Crisis management plans (Chapter 8)

You might feel that this is all a huge task. There's no rush. If you would like some support, I'm always here to help. DM me on social media (you can find me on LinkedIn, Facebook, Instagram, Twitter and TikTok @luanwise) or email: sayhello@luanwise.co.uk.

Additional resources

Throughout the book, you will find references to further reading, including books, research papers, videos and websites.

These are also summarised at the end of this book and can be found by visiting my website at www.luanwise.co.uk/books/planning-for-success or scanning the QR code below.

For marketing educators, on the website page, you can find links to request teaching materials, including PowerPoint slides and topical discussion guides. I always welcome opportunities to meet students and deliver guest lectures.

Chapter 1

Understanding the ever-changing social media landscape

In this chapter, we will:

- Gain an understanding of the history and evolution of social media.
- Find out about the different activities social media is used for.
- Establish the role of social media marketing in the buying decision process.

While you read this page, 21 million people will be actively using Facebook, 2 million Snapchats will be sent, 66 thousand photos and videos will be shared on Instagram, and 167 million videos will be watched on TikTok (Local IQ, 2022).

How does that make you feel? Excited to be part of the social media world, or overwhelmed by the number of platforms and the volume of content?

Whatever you might think or feel about social media, it is now very much part of our everyday lives. The average internet user aged 16–64 uses

7.2 social platforms, via 2.7 devices, spending 2 hours 31 minutes a day on social media (DataReportal, January 2023).

Even if you are not a regular user, you will likely hear about what's happening on social media via other media, or from friends, family and colleagues. And there's no doubt that social media is a hugely powerful communications channel, enabling users to access information, share ideas, create connections, networks and communities, send messages, and be entertained.

The ubiquity of social media in our lives has occurred over a relatively short period, especially when compared to the adoption of other media. The telephone took 75 years to reach 50 million users, radio took 38 years, and television took 13 years. By contrast, the World Wide Web, created in 1989, had 50 million users only four years later. By 2000, around 100 million people had access to the internet, and it was common for people to engage socially online. Facebook reached 50 million users within two years of its launch and Twitter took just nine months. You can see this in Figure 1.1. As this book goes to press (July 2023), Instagram's new app, Threads, launched and reached 50 million users in less than 48 hours.

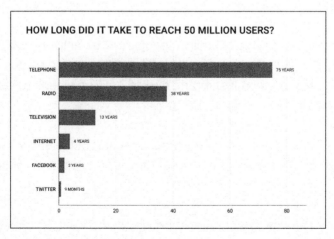

Figure 1.1. How long each form of media took to reach 50 million users.

Just as the invention of television changed media consumption from listening (radio) to watching, social media has created both media producers and content creators. It is now possible for anyone to create and share content, from anywhere, at any time – and it is also possible to consume content from anywhere, at any time. We no longer rely on media companies, or even celebrities, to shape and control the information we receive.

Figure 1.2 shows a timeline of key events in the world of social media.

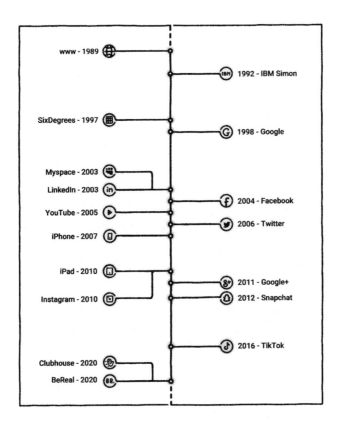

Figure 1.2. Social media timeline (1989–2020).

The growth of both social media platforms and users can be closely attributed to developments in web technologies, most notably the introduction of the smartphone.

When IBM showcased the IBM Simon at the 1992 COMDEX (Computer Dealers' Exhibition), it was the first time that telephony and personal computing had been combined. The Blackberry gained mass popularity in 2006, but then Apple introduced the iPhone in 2007 – one of the first smartphones to use a touchscreen interface. Today, there are more than 1.5 billion active iPhone users worldwide. (It is interesting to note that Apple is only responsible for about 13% of the global market share for smartphone devices; Android is the most popular operating system.) The launch of the iPad in 2010, a tablet-style computer, was another technology game changer.

Not all social media platforms have survived. Six Degrees, launched in 1997 and considered to be the first social network, enabled users to upload a profile and make friends with other users. Its growth was limited due to the low number of people connected to the internet at the time, and it closed in 2001. Myspace was the largest social networking site from 2005–2008 when Facebook overtook it.

Defining social media

There appears to be no universally agreed definition of social media. For the purposes of our research study, and this book, social media is: 'an umbrella term that defines the various activities that integrate technology, social interaction and the construction of words, video, and audio.'

The social media map created by Overdrive Interactive lists over 650 platforms, tools, applications and resources for social media marketing. You can access it at www.ovrdrv.com/knowledge/social-media-map.

Understanding change in social media

Each year, new platforms and apps are launched, and others decline. Some become mainstream, while others find their key features being copied by the dominant players and the initial interest in something new is then lost.

Understanding trends in social media and the use of platforms is essential for organisations, content creators and individuals alike. By staying informed and adapting to change when necessary, we can make the most of social media's capacity to act as a powerful tool for connection, communication and engagement.

In my first book, *Relax! It's Only Social Media*, I discussed the importance of Google+. It closed down in 2019. According to Google, this was due to low usage and lack of user engagement.

Clubhouse, an audio-only app, launched in 2020, during the Covid-19 pandemic, as an invite-only iPhone app – perfect at a time when people were fatigued by being on-screen with Zoom/Microsoft Teams. It quickly reached 10 million downloads in February 2021 but then fell out of popularity just as quickly – especially since, when the euphoria died down, invites were no longer needed to download it, and when other social media platforms, such as Twitter, announced their own audio-only feature (Twitter Spaces).

BeReal, launched in 2020, won the iPhone App of the Year award in 2022 for giving people 'an authentic glimpse into their friends and family's everyday lives.' However, at the time of writing this in early

2023, it is starting to see a significant decline in downloads. The any-time-of-day notification to take a photo that includes a selfie and rear-facing photo melded together in a single post has been copied by TikTok (as TikTok Now) and Instagram (as Candid). This is another example of a single-feature app having an instant novelty appeal to social media users, with the bigger players copying it as soon as they can and users sticking to an app where they have more history, content and followers. (Interestingly, TikTok Now was discontinued in June 2023).

For business leaders and marketers, understanding what's happening in the world of social media, at both a strategic and a tactical level, is critical to developing and implementing effective marketing and communications strategies. However, while new social media platforms and features may be exciting and hold promise, it's important to approach them with a critical eye, consider the potential benefits and risks, and make a judgement that aligns with the behaviours of your target audience, the needs of your business, and your available resources. Keep reading, and by the end of the book, you will have the know-how to make these assessments.

Do you suffer from shiny object syndrome?

Shiny object syndrome is a term used to describe the tendency for people to be easily distracted by new, attractive ideas, tools or technologies, instead of focusing on what they have been working on or what they have already established as a goal. In the context of social media marketing, it refers to the constant distraction marketers face due to the ever-changing landscape of the platforms and the emergence of new features.

People who suffer from shiny object syndrome tend to constantly switch their focus from one tactic to another. This can result in

---

ineffective use of resources and a lack of consistent progress towards marketing objectives.

Throughout this book, we will be focusing on making informed decisions. If you find yourself distracted, put on your thinking cap and use your objectives to keep you on track. A new feature might impact your tactics, but it should not change your final destination. It's likely that you will also want to test something new before making a big change.

'Most things in life are cyclical, and understanding prior cycles that you've been in helps you to understand and predict trends of the future.'

Andy Lambert

I co-host a monthly webinar that covers all the changes happening in social media with Andy Lambert, and there's always plenty to talk about.

Andy was part of the founding team of ContentCal, a social media marketing Software as a Service (SaaS) product. Over five years, they raised over $10 million, grew to be used by thousands of customers in over 100 countries, and won numerous awards. At the end of 2021, they were acquired by Adobe Inc. Andy and I connected through the content we share on social media.

Together, we discuss hot topics and what they might mean in practice, aiming to help others cut through the noise and stay up to date by summarising new data and the latest trends, and identifying which feature changes are positive moves, and perhaps which areas are not so important. We're always clear that it's OK to be an earlier adopter and try new things out, but it's also OK to wait and see what others are doing before diving in.

Additional resources

To ensure you're always in the know when it comes to the latest social media news and trends, take a look at my one-stop social media news and resource website, www.thelighthouse. social. You can subscribe to weekly email updates and receive information about monthly webinars and other events.

An introduction to LinkedIn, Twitter, Facebook, Instagram, TikTok and Snapchat

It would be impossible to write a book about all the social media platforms available, so we will focus on the social media platforms I discuss most often with my consultancy and training clients. They are:

- LinkedIn
- Twitter
- Facebook
- Instagram
- TikTok
- Snapchat

Please note that this is not a recommendation for the platforms I think you should use (we'll go through that decision-making process later). By the time you read this, some platforms might no longer exist, and new platforms might have launched. However, I'm confident that the principles discussed throughout this book can be applied to any social media platform, and the additional resources provided will direct you to the latest news and data to inform any decisions you need to make as part of your social media marketing planning.

So, by way of an introduction, let's look at the mission statements and some key features of each of these platforms.

LinkedIn

LinkedIn is a business and employment-focused social media platform. It officially launched to the public on 5 May 2003 with the mission to 'connect the world's professionals to make them more productive and successful'. Its vision is to 'create economic opportunity for every professional'.

By 2005, LinkedIn had more than a million users. By 2011, when it became a publicly traded company, it had more than 90 million members and was available in eight languages. In 2016 LinkedIn was purchased by Microsoft for $26.2 billion. In 2023, LinkedIn has more than 950 million members in 200 countries and regions worldwide.

LinkedIn is made up of personal profiles and company Pages. Personal profiles are created by individuals where they describe their career story, employment history and education details.

By connecting with others on LinkedIn, individual users build up a professional network of contacts comprising 1st, 2nd- and 3rd-degree connections:

- 1st-degree: People you're directly connected to because you have accepted their invitation to connect, or they have accepted your invitation.
- 2nd-degree: People who are connected to your 1st-degree connections.

- 3rd-degree: People who are connected to your 2nd-degree connections.

Once a user makes a 1st-degree connection, that user sees their new connection's information updates in their home page newsfeed and notifications. People who are 1st-degree connections can also send direct (private) messages to each other. More recently, LinkedIn has added the option to 'follow' individual users. Following lets users see another LinkedIn member's activity in their newsfeed without connecting to them.

Organisations and educational institutions represent themselves on LinkedIn by setting up a Page and sharing information that helps people to learn more about the organisation, its products/services and career opportunities. Employees connect themselves to their employer's company Page through the 'Experience' section of their personal profiles.

LinkedIn Groups are online communities within the LinkedIn platform where professionals with similar interests, industries, or affiliations can connect, share knowledge, and engage in discussions. These groups provide a valuable space for networking, learning from industry peers, and exchanging insights on specific topics.

Additional resources

Visit www.luanwise.co.uk/books/linkedin-success to find my e-book *LinkedIn Success: The Ultimate Guide to Perfecting Your Profile*. The e-book includes links to 'how to' videos that are regularly updated.

Twitter

At the time of going to print, Twitter has announced a rebrand to X. As the terminology of Twitter, Tweet, ReTweet etc is well-known and understood I have not changed the following text. I hope you will be able to swap out the relevant words if required.

Founded in 2006, Twitter's mission is 'to give everyone the power to create and share ideas and information instantly, without barriers'. Twitter declares its platform to be a place for sharing 'what is happening in the world and what people are talking about right now', including breaking news, entertainment, sports, politics and everyday interests.

It enables users to post short updates, known as Tweets, to their followers. Tweets were initially limited to 140 characters, then in 2017, they were extended to 280 characters. Tweets can be text, GIF, photo or video. Unlike connecting on LinkedIn, following users on Twitter does not need to be reciprocal.

Every second, on average, there are around 6,000 new Tweets. It's a fast and sometimes furious platform for information and opinion-sharing.

In addition to short-form posts, Twitter has some key features called Spaces and Communities.

In November 2020, Twitter Spaces was launched as a live audio-only chatroom feature. The creator of a Space is the host, who can send requests to listeners to become co-hosts or speakers. Anyone can join as a listener, including people who don't follow the Space's creator.

In 2021, Twitter launched Communities to give people a dedicated place to connect, share, and get closer to the discussions they care about most. Communities are started, administered and moderated by Twitter users who enforce Community rules and keep conversations informative, relevant and fun. People who accept invitations to join a Community become members. Tweets in Communities can be seen by anyone on Twitter, but only people within the Community can participate in the discussion.

2022 was an interesting year for Twitter, with a $44-billion acquisition by South African-born American entrepreneur Elon Musk. Musk, a co-founder of PayPal, founder of SpaceX (a company that makes rockets and spacecraft) and early funder of Tesla (a company that makes electric cars and batteries) made immediate changes to the platform and, at the time of writing, continues to do so. Launching a Twitter Blue subscription model is just one example – this currently includes the opportunity to upload longer videos, write longer Tweets (up to 25,000 characters), edit a Tweet, and view fewer advertisements.

For the first time in its history, new profile types are also becoming available, including an option for organisations.

Facebook

Facebook was launched in 2004 as a social networking service for Harvard University students and was introduced to the UK in 2005, again targeted at students. It opened to the public in September 2006, and since then has provided unprecedented insights into people's lives and psychology. It has also been at the heart of controversy from data scandals to election-rigging.

Facebook's first stated mission was 'to give people the power to share and make the world more open and connected'. In 2017 the statement was updated to 'give people the power to build community and bring the world closer together', providing a positive outcome to the idea of connection.

In 2021, the company rebranded as Meta. CEO Mark Zuckerberg said that the existing brand could not 'possibly represent everything that we're doing today, let alone in the future'. This was, in part, due to Zuckerberg's focus on the next evolution of social connection and his vision for bringing the metaverse to life. Meta comes from the Greek word for 'beyond', and for Zuckerberg, the word shows that there is always more to build.

On the Facebook platform, individuals have 'profiles', and they connect with others who are known as 'friends'. At the time of writing, Facebook is rolling out a professional mode for profiles: a setting that provides opportunities for creators to monetise their profiles. Organisations have 'pages' and can build followers through both organic and paid-for content.

In October 2010, Facebook launched groups – digital communities where users interact with like-minded individuals. By January 2016 Facebook groups had more than 1 billion users. Zuckerberg has frequently shared Facebook's focus on groups as a meaningful social infrastructure and updated the platform to prioritise showing content from groups in users' timelines.

In January 2023 Facebook was listed as the world's most-used social media platform, with over 2.9 billion monthly active users worldwide; 67% of those users log in daily. As a comparison, Facebook's active user base is larger than the populations of China and India combined.

Additional resources

If you want to know more about Facebook, I recommend watching the film *The Social Network* and reading Steven Levy's book *Facebook: The Inside Story*.

Instagram

Instagram launched in October 2010 as a photo- and video-sharing app with the mission 'to capture and share the world's moments'. Facebook acquired Instagram for $1 billion in September 2012, and it became part of the Facebook (now Meta) family of apps, which now also includes WhatsApp (acquired in 2014).

In July 2021 the head of Instagram, Adam Mosseri, announced via his personal profile (@mosseri) that Instagram was 'no longer a square photo-sharing app'. He also mentioned the stiff competition from TikTok and YouTube in providing entertaining content via video.

By mid-2022 the shift towards video content saw a backlash from its highest-profile users, Kim Kardashian and Kylie Jenner, who complained that 'it was trying to be TikTok' instead of focusing on photo sharing. They asked the company to 'make Instagram Instagram again'. Mosseri and his colleagues listened, acknowledged the feedback, and made some immediate reversals to changes they had been experimenting with.

In 2023, Instagram boasts 2 billion monthly active users and high popularity among younger audiences (those aged 18–34 make up over 60% of Instagram's user base).

Additional resources

To learn more about Instagram, check out *No Filter: The Inside Story of Instagram* by Sarah Frier.

TikTok

TikTok allows users to create and share short-form videos set to music, sound bites or other audio snippets.

With a mission to inspire creativity and bring joy, TikTok was launched in September 2016 by the Chinese tech company ByteDance under the name Douyin. In November 2017, ByteDance acquired another social media app called Musical.ly, which allowed users to create and share 15-second lip-sync videos on their platform. ByteDance eventually closed the Musical.ly app and incorporated most of its features into Douyin. In August 2018, ByteDance released the global version of Douyin – TikTok.

Downloads of TikTok accelerated significantly during the Covid-19 lockdowns: during the week of 23 March 2020, when the UK lockdown was enforced, UK downloads surged by 34%. Instead of going out, Britons stayed in and whiled away time on TikTok.

In Matthew Brennan's self-published book, *Attention Factory: The Story of TikTok and China's ByteDance (p. 111)*, he shares interesting insights into the growth of the platform:

In trying to encourage a sense of community amongst their early adopters, the team discovered that the most effective way was to regularly promote 'challenges'. ...A challenge sets up a replicable, cookie-cutter structure that allows anyone to take part and make their own version.

By providing direction, TikTok lowered the entry barrier to content creation; it had recognised that the 'most significant barrier to people creating videos wasn't a technical one'. It also wasn't a problem of shyness: 'The more substantial barrier was one of creativity and inspiration.' The nature of the challenges set inspired its audiences – and also created FOMO in users, who didn't want to miss out on getting involved with a new trend.

This insight about encouraging your audience to participate (and making it easy) is invaluable, and one to remember when you're planning your own social media content.

TikTok is a platform for users who want to watch funny or entertaining content. According to a report by Hootsuite (Social Media Trends 2023), only 33.9% of TikTok users publish content to the platform; in comparison, 69.9% of Instagram users publish their own photos and videos.

Like on other social media platforms, you can follow users on TikTok, but most TikTok users will also browse the 'For You' section, which shows users content based on their past activity. TikToks with good user engagement (likes, shares, watch time) will be pushed to more users with similar interests. This process occurs regardless of how many followers the account has, which follows TikTok's philosophy that if the content is good, it will travel far.

Snapchat

Snapchat is a multimedia messaging app that was launched in 2011 by Evan Spiegel, Bobby Murphy and Reggie Brown, students at

Stanford University. The app quickly gained popularity for its unique approach to communication: it emphasises ephemeral messaging – messages and media that disappear after being viewed.

Snapchat's mission statement is to 'empower people to express themselves, live in the moment, learn about the world, and have fun together'. The app achieves this by offering a range of features that allow users to capture and share photos and videos, chat with friends, and play games.

Snapchat was the first platform to introduce Stories (in 2013), which allow users to create a sequence of photos and videos that disappear after 24 hours. Yes, this feature is now part of Instagram (launched in 2016) and Facebook (launched in 2017). LinkedIn also trialled Stories in 2020 but removed them a year later.

In 2015 Snapchat introduced filters – digital effects and overlays that can be added to photos and videos taken within the app. Since the introduction of Lenses (the first filter), Snapchat has expanded its filter offerings, including Geofilters, which are location-based overlays that can be added to snaps taken within a specific geographic area, and Bitmoji filters, which allow users to add personalised Bitmoji stickers to their snaps.

Snapchat filters have been so popular that other social media platforms have created their own versions of filters.

Do you see a pattern emerging here? If there's anything we might predict about the future of social media, it's that there will be common features across all platforms – we just need to see who's first to come up with something new!

A note about YouTube

While YouTube is a popular and widely used platform for sharing videos and engaging with content creators, it is not typically considered a social media platform like those described above. This is because, unlike Facebook, Instagram and LinkedIn, where the primary focus is on building a social network and sharing content with friends, family and professional connections, YouTube has primarily been a content distribution platform. While users can comment on videos and interact with creators, the social aspect of YouTube is secondary to its primary purpose of sharing and discovering video content.

However, in 2020 YouTube introduced YouTube Shorts, a short-form video feature, as a response to the popularity of TikTok and Reels. Like TikTok and Reels on Instagram and Facebook, YouTube Shorts includes a range of editing tools and music options that allow creators to add effects, text and music to their videos. The feature also includes a personalised feed that recommends Shorts to viewers based on their viewing history and interests and a dedicated Shorts tab on the YouTube app for easy discovery.

It's interesting to consider why, if social media platforms have such similar features, the average internet user is active on multiple platforms – and in turn, why organisations need to have a presence on multiple platforms.

First, different platforms may have distinct user demographics, so individuals may join multiple platforms to connect with different social circles or target specific audiences. Second, each platform may offer unique content or experiences, such as visual-centric content on Instagram or professional networking on LinkedIn, prompting users to diversify their social media presence for different purposes.

Findings from DataReportal (January 2023) highlight that 78.9% of TikTok users are looking for funny or entertaining content, versus 33.5% using the platform to keep up to date with news and current events. LinkedIn users, however, are mostly looking for news and researching brands and products; only 13.6% of social media users go to LinkedIn for funny or entertaining content.

Case study: Xero, Serial Killer Receipts

If you are unsure about creating funny or entertaining content for your business, here's an award-winning case study from accountancy software provider, Xero, showing how it can be done.

Their 'Serial Killer Receipts' tactical campaign won the Gold Muse Award for Social Media – Humour in 2023. The campaign focused on engaging with accountants and bookkeepers during Halloween. Recognising the aversion accountants have towards paper receipts, the campaign aimed to create a sense of fear, amusement and community for the target audience. The campaign featured carefully crafted social posts showcasing fictional receipts inspired by famous horror movie killers such as Freddy Krueger. Each post included elements from traditional receipts, combined with movie trivia and dry humour.

Released over a 24-hour period, the posts included questions for the audience, encouraging them to identify the receipt owner, determine tax deductibles and reconcile expenses. The intention was to provide accountants and bookkeepers with moments of

---

light-hearted relief amid their preparations for tax season while positioning the brand as one that understands their sense of humour and values a human-centric approach.

You can view the award-winning campaign creative at: www. museaward.com/winner-info.php?id=224435

The marketing funnel

When you consider making a purchase, you will go through a series of thoughts, evaluations and comparisons before arriving at a decision. This is true for both personal purchases and purchases you might be involved with at work. It can take just a few moments for a simple purchase, such as a food snack or stationery item, or it can take longer for something of greater value, such as a new home or customer relationship management (CRM) software.

In 1968, Engel, Kollat and Blackwell, in their book *Consumer Behavior*, developed a model that explains the series of steps we go through when purchasing a product or service: problem/need recognition, information search, evaluation of alternatives, purchase decision, and post-purchase evaluation.

Figure 1.3 shows these steps as a funnel. It's shown as a funnel because of the numbers (individuals or organisations) involved at each stage. Early in the process, there may be many more individuals or organisational buyers that show interest in your products or services. For various reasons, not all of these buyers will progress through the journey to buying from your organisation. They might decide to purchase elsewhere, or they might not have the budget they need to buy from you. We commonly use the term 'journey' because it signifies that the process involves multiple stages and interactions, or 'touchpoints'.

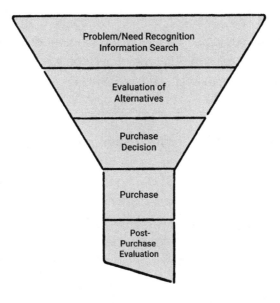

Figure 1.3. The buying decision process shown as a marketing funnel.

A potential customer begins their journey to purchase your product or service by recognising that they have a problem. At times, individuals may not realise they have a problem until they come across your social media content!

You might have heard a quote attributed to Henry Ford: 'If I had asked people what they wanted, they would have said a faster horse.' They didn't know about cars, so they didn't know they wanted one. Your potential customer may not be aware of your products or services, and how these could make their lives better. To embrace this principle in social media marketing, focus on not just showcasing your products or services, but also education and engaging your audience about the problems your offerings solve and the benefits they bring, thereby helping them realise their unmet needs and desires.

Once a problem has been recognised, there is an information search stage. A potential customer will be looking for more detail to help them decide to buy (or not). After they have completed an information search, they will begin to evaluate alternatives.

B2B vs B2C marketing – a brief summary

Business-to-consumer (B2C) buying is often done by an individual for a low-value item. Bigger decisions, such as an annual holiday, might take more time and will include the whole family. Many B2C products are purchased via a third party, for example, a retailer, with the customer having no direct relationship with the organisation.

Most business-to-business (B2B) products and services are purchased direct or via an approved reseller. B2B buying can often include six or more people as part of the decision-making unit within an organisation. B2B buying is often considered to be more rational than B2C, but emotion is key in B2B too. Although the individual is not spending their own money, people don't want to make a bad decision that could upset colleagues and potentially put their job at risk. It's why the classic 'you won't get fired for buying IBM' quote is often cited.

After the evaluation of alternatives, it's (hopefully) time for the purchase decision to be made.

But the process does not end with the purchase. Customers will evaluate whether they have made the right decision, and if they have, they will advocate for you – with a positive review and recommendations.

Figure 1.4 shows the social media marketing tasks associated with each stage of the buying decision process.

Figure 1.4. The social media marketing tasks associated with the buying decision process.

The stages of the marketing task are commonly referred to as AIDA: Awareness, Interest, Desire and Action. It's another marketing classic;

US psychologist Edward Kellogg Strong, Jr first referred to AIDA in 1925. The model refers to:

- **Awareness:** The first step is to capture the attention of the target audience. You need to let people know that your organisation exists and introduce your products and services to them.
- **Interest:** Once you have their attention, the next step is to generate interest, to pique their curiosity and make them want to learn more about you and your organisation.
- **Desire:** After building interest, the next task is to create a desire for your products or services.
- **Action:** The final stage of the AIDA model is to prompt the audience to take an action, i.e. make a purchase.

When our new customers are evaluating their purchase, the social media marketing task continues, with the need to create loyalty and advocacy.

It's clear to see that social media has a role to play at every stage, due to its combination of reach, interactivity and real-time engagement. This is not true for other marketing channels, such as print advertising or email marketing, which are more likely to be most effective at just one or two of the stages of the funnel.

The social media marketing challenge is to maintain visibility as potential customers progress through their buying decision process. Research has shown that often the organisation/individual that has been most visible and helpful throughout their buying journey tends to be successful. By staying at the forefront of customers' minds and facilitating a path of least resistance, organisations increase the likelihood of conversion and winning the sale.

Every social media post that gets seen by your target audience will help guide them through their journey to making a purchase decision.

Our research asked marketers to identify the role of different social media platforms in relation to elements of the marketing funnel. Figure 1.5 shows that in 2020 and 2022 Facebook was seen by our research respondents to be the platform most used to increase awareness. Facebook is closely followed by Twitter and Instagram, then LinkedIn. There was a drop in the use of LinkedIn and Facebook for awareness between 2020 and 2022, alongside an increase in the use of Twitter, Snapchat and TikTok. We can clearly see that the biggest change (increase) is the use of TikTok, which is supported by a growth in the number of users over the same time period.

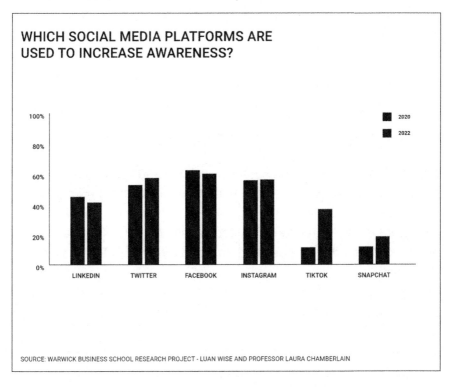

WHICH SOCIAL MEDIA PLATFORMS ARE USED TO INCREASE AWARENESS?

SOURCE: WARWICK BUSINESS SCHOOL RESEARCH PROJECT - LUAN WISE AND PROFESSOR LAURA CHAMBERLAIN

Figure 1.5. The social media platforms used to increase awareness.

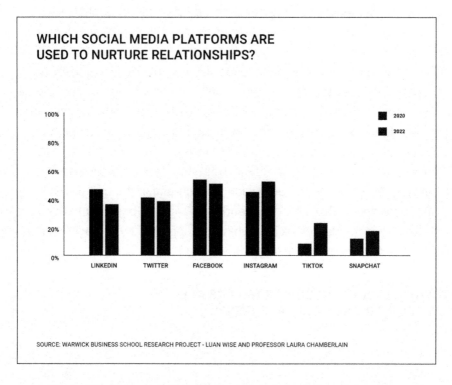

WHICH SOCIAL MEDIA PLATFORMS ARE
USED TO NURTURE RELATIONSHIPS?

SOURCE: WARWICK BUSINESS SCHOOL RESEARCH PROJECT - LUAN WISE AND PROFESSOR LAURA CHAMBERLAIN

Figure 1.6. The social media platforms used to nurture relationships.

Further down the marketing funnel, Facebook and Instagram again lead the way in being used to nurture relationships (Figure 1.6). Between 2020 and 2022 there was a shift from Facebook to Instagram. There's an interesting decrease in the role of Twitter and LinkedIn for this purpose and an increase for both TikTok and Snapchat.

At both stages, there is a role for each of the social media platforms.

This snapshot shows just how things can change over a short time, and how there isn't a single answer to this question; it's different for every organisation. This is something you will need to consider as you build your one-page social media marketing plan and content calendar.

Additional resources

The marketing funnel is key to every business. If you are thinking that there must be a way to keep more people in your marketing funnel throughout the process, you are correct. However, that is outside the scope of this book. *Watertight Marketing: The Proven Process for Seriously Scaleable Sales* by Bryony Thomas is a methodology based on addressing key touchpoint leaks, and I highly recommend you add this book to your reading list.

If you're looking for a more detailed framework for understanding the customer experience at every touchpoint throughout the buying decision process, you should explore customer journey mapping.

I recommend reading *The Journey Mapping Playbook: A Practical Guide to Preparing, Facilitating and Unlocking the Value of Customer Journey Mapping* by Jerry Angrave.

Chapter summary

In this first chapter, we have reviewed a brief history of social media to give context to the ever-changing landscape and help us understand how to embrace the ongoing changes. We have reviewed the mission statements and key features of some of the most used social media platforms (globally). We now know the stages of the buying decision process and the role of social media marketing at each stage.

Actions

- Visit www.thelighthouse.social or scan the QR code below to subscribe to email updates for the latest news and event information.
- Reviewing industry award winners provides valuable insights into successful approaches. You might also consider entering your own campaigns for awards! Look at the B2B Marketing Awards (https://events.b2bmarketing.net/b2bawards), Chartered Institute of Marketing Excellence Awards (https://www.cim.co.uk/global-marketing-excellence-awards/), Chartered Institute of Public Relations Excellence Awards (www.cipr.co.uk), The Drum Social Buzz Awards (www.thedrumawards.com) and the Global and UK Social Media Awards (https://dontpanicprojects.com/our-awards/). A full list of UK business awards can be found at www.awards-list.co.uk.

Chapter 2

Setting meaningful social media goals and objectives

In this chapter, we will:

- Discover the difference between strategy and tactics.
- Recognise the importance of purpose and values.
- Learn how to set SMART objectives.

Imagine a world where every social media post you create has intention, every comment you leave sparks a thoughtful conversation, and every follower you gain represents a genuine connection. This might sound unlikely, but it can happen if you set meaningful social media goals and objectives.

Social media has the power to elevate a business's brand, engage its audience, and drive conversions; these are the desired actions taken by the audience, such as making a purchase, signing up for a newsletter or filling out a contact form. However, without clear guidance for content creation and community management, there is a risk of being inefficient, wasting valuable resources and time on activities that fail to resonate with your target audience – and ultimately hinder your desired conversions.

What is social media community management?

Community management is the process of engaging audiences across social media platforms to increase brand loyalty and grow authentic connections.

Community managers play a crucial role in representing the organisation's voice and values, responding to comments and messages, and acting as facilitators for positive conversations and engagements.

Meta offers an online course and certification in community management. Find out more at www.facebook.com/business/learn

---

When aiming to influence purchasing decisions through social media marketing, it is important to concentrate on desired outcomes and stimulating changes in behaviour, i.e. impacts, rather than getting caught up in specific outputs or quantity of social media posts.

For example, a software company might aim to generate qualified leads for their enterprise solution. Instead of solely measuring the number of social media posts or followers, the focus is on driving tangible outcomes such as lead conversions and pipeline growth. Marketing activities would involve creating content that addresses pain points and showcases the benefits of the software solution, utilising social media advertising to reach relevant decision-makers in the target industry, and tracking the number of qualified leads generated. By prioritising the outcome of lead generation and pipeline growth, the software company can assess the effectiveness of their social media efforts in driving valuable business opportunities.

In the absence of clear outcomes navigating social media for business can be like driving without a reliable satnav system – without a destination in mind, any path might seem plausible, but there's no guarantee that you will get where you want to go. As the author of *Alice in Wonderland*, Lewis Carroll, famously said: 'If you don't know where you're going, any road will get you there.'

Goals are the broad, overarching statements that define the desired outcome of your social media marketing efforts. They provide a sense of direction and purpose for your activity. Goals are typically long-term and focus on the big picture.

Objectives are more specific, measurable and time-bound than goals. They serve as stepping stones towards achieving your broader goals. We'll learn how to set objectives later in this chapter.

Strategy vs tactics

Strategy is a term that, I believe, is vastly overused. For me, strategy guides your overall approach, and tactics are specific actions you take to achieve the strategy.

We should always start at the top with the overall business strategy. This includes the vision, mission and 'big picture' view of an organisation. Each function within an organisation, from human resources to operations, finance and marketing will then define their own strategy to outline how they will help to achieve the overall business strategy.

Once a strategy has been agreed, it paves the way for developing a comprehensive plan that outlines the specific actions, or tactics, timelines, and resources required to achieve the strategy.

The plan will include the selection of which platforms to use, and implementation of various tactics such as content formats, influencer collaborations, paid advertising campaigns, strategic hashtag usage, and so on.

You are likely to need always-on plans to encompass business-as-usual activity, and sometimes additional campaign-specific plans. These may be time-specific, such as a campaign to support a product sales promotion, or the release of a new podcast, for example.

There must be strong alignment between strategy and tactics. This is the biggest mistake I see with social media – diving straight into tactics. And not just when there is a new and shiny feature or trend to consider, but overall. How many times have you had conversations at work about 'setting up a new Instagram account', without discussing how that might align with your overarching strategy?

Without alignment, we could fail to achieve our business goals and objectives. We could waste valuable resources and become busy fools. However, as the comment below from one of our qualitative research interviews shows, it's all too common for social media to be an 'add-on' activity rather than fully integrated into business and marketing planning.

> **Social media is tacked onto the end of marketing activity. It's very much 'Oh yeah, make sure that goes out on LinkedIn'.**

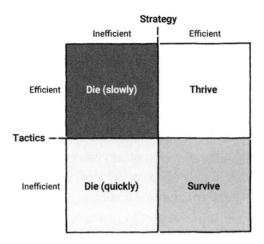

Figure 2.1. The strategy vs tactics matrix.

The strategy vs tactics matrix is shown in Figure 2.1. This is a tool used to differentiate between doing the right things (strategy) and doing things right (tactics).

The matrix is divided into four quadrants:

- **Thrive:** This is the most desirable quadrant, where both strategies and tactics are efficient.
- **Survive:** A business can survive with an efficient strategy and inefficient tactics. In this quadrant, a business will achieve its objectives but may use more resources than necessary, or struggle to grow or compete with more efficient competitors.
- **Die (Slowly):** With an inefficient strategy but efficient tactics, a business will struggle. It needs to adjust its strategy.
- **Die (Quickly):** This is clearly the least desirable quadrant – when both tactics and strategy are inefficient, organisations are likely to fail and die quickly.

In Figure 2.2 we can see that just over half (56.2%) of the people we surveyed in 2020 said they understood how social media fitted into the business plan. Almost one-third (31.6%) stated that they did not understand how social media fitted into their organisation's business plan, and 12.3% were unsure. Two years later, we see a shift of uncertainty from 12.3% to 7.9% of respondents who 'neither agree or disagree' with the same question.

It's essential to align social media objectives with the overall business plan. My experience in delivering social media training has shown that there is often a lack of communication about the business plan, so alignment (or not) could be due to a lack of knowledge about the plan when setting social media objectives. Understanding your organisation's big-picture strategy, and asking to see the business plan when building your social media marketing plan is critical.

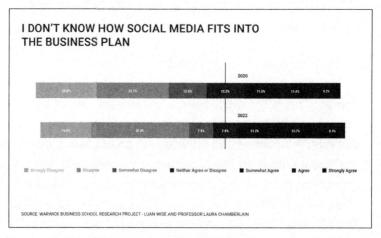

Figure 2.2. Responses to the statement, 'I don't know how social media fits into the business plan.'

Finding your purpose

> *'People don't buy what you do, they buy why you do it.'*
> Simon Sinek

Before we consider how to set social media marketing objectives, make a tea or coffee, whichever you prefer, and search for Simon Sinek's 'Start with Why' TED Talk on YouTube.

Sinek says that every organisation functions on three levels:

1. What we do.
2. How we do it.
3. Why we do it.

He argues that every organisation knows what it does – the products it sells or services it offers, and every individual knows what they do – their job title and responsibilities.

Some also know how they do what they do, and what they think makes them different from everyone else. However, Sinek continues, few people and organisations can clearly articulate why they do what they do – and why that should matter to anyone else. Yet when organisations, and people, know their why, they enjoy greater long-term success, command greater trust and loyalty among employees and customers, and are more forward-thinking and innovative than their competition.

Sinek calls this concept the 'Golden Circle' (Figure 2.3). Most of the time, we communicate from the outside in. We start with what we do, then how we do it. When we meet new customers, the first thing most of us tell them is what we do, then we explain how we do it or how we are different.

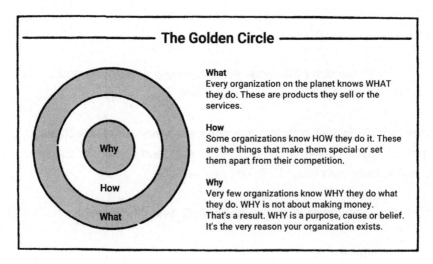

The Golden Circle

What
Every organization on the planet knows WHAT they do. These are products they sell or the services.

How
Some organizations know HOW they do it. These are the things that make them special or set them apart from their competition.

Why
Very few organizations know WHY they do what they do. WHY is not about making money. That's a result. WHY is a purpose, cause or belief. It's the very reason your organization exists.

Why

How

What

Figure 2.3. The Golden Circle. Image reproduced with permission from the author.

In her must-read book, *Marketing: A Love Story: How to Matter to Your Customers (p. 26)*, Bernadette Jiwa summarises the limitations of 'how':

Nobody told Jobs and Wozniak how to build a computer company, let alone how to make it one of the most loved brands in the world, and Howard Schultz didn't get the Starbucks magic from a manual.

Nobody can tell you what to stand for, or how your values, wants and needs should intersect with those of your customer and then manifest as an idea or an experience. Figuring out the destination is hard – but recognising it is more valuable than knowing exactly how you're going to get there. Until you do the hard work of understanding the 'why' and the 'who for', every tactical 'how to' has the potential to take you down the wrong track.

If a decision-maker is asked why they chose one product or service over another, they will often cite features, benefits, facts or figures, because the neocortex, the thinking part of the brain, is always trying to understand and make sense of the world. This is why we think we are rational beings when we really are not. People understand factual information – but this understanding does not drive behaviour. We would not be loyal; we would always choose the best deal. We would not care about trust or relationships; we would only evaluate the numbers. But we don't do that. We choose a product, service or organisation because of the way it makes us feel.

When we communicate from the inside out, starting with why, communication starts to drive decision-making and behaviour, attracting people with reciprocal beliefs and who want to be a part of the same cause.

Sinek uses Apple as an example during his TED Talk, demonstrating their Golden Circle as follows:

Why: everything we do, we believe in challenging the status quo. We believe in thinking differently.

How: the way we challenge the status quo is by making our products beautifully designed, simple to use, and user-friendly.

What: we just happen to make great computers.

Consider the last big purchase you made.

Why did you select that organisation and their product or service?

For the Golden Circle to work properly you must be clear about why, be disciplined about how and be consistent about what. No section is more important than the others. Aim for a balance across all three.

When an individual or organisation is clear about its 'why', everyone, from employees to customers, can understand it.

Your 'why' is the purpose, cause or belief that drives everything you do. It's what sets you apart from your competitors and helps you to attract customers who share a similar worldview.

Brand purpose and ethical, sustainable values are a priority in both B2C and B2B spheres. According to the *'Creating Epic Customer Experiences'* report by Marketo (2019), over two-thirds (68%) of B2B buyers surveyed said that brand purpose is important during the buying decision process: two-thirds (67%) strive to work with brands with strong environmental credentials, and 64% are more likely to consider organisations that demonstrate fair, ethical practices throughout their supply chain. Nearly half (48%) of B2B marketers reported lost sales because of unclear brand values and purpose. A third of business buyers (30%) said they would walk away if a brand's values seemed at odds with theirs.

Customers that are not connected to your purpose will purchase from you because they *need* to, not necessarily because they *want* to. However, they are more likely to be loyal to your brand, trust you, buy other products and services, and act as advocates of your organisation if they share your purpose.

What do values and purpose mean to Generation Z?

Research shows that each generation has its own unique values, preferences and experiences that shape their buying behaviour and decision-making. You may find that generation features as part of your customer personas, and that your

---

social media plans and activity will be influenced by their characteristics. We will be looking at customer personas in Chapter 3.

Entering the workplace for the first time, with huge influence and buying power, is Generation Z (Gen Z for short) – people born between the mid-1990s and early-2010s. As the first generation to grow up in a fully digital age, Gen Z has a unique perspective on life and work, and they prioritise purpose and meaning more than any other generation before them.

Gen Z has grown up in a world of change, uncertainty and disruption. They have seen the effects of climate change, economic inequality and political polarisation, and they are deeply concerned about the future. As a result, they are seeking purpose and meaning in their lives and careers, and they are looking for organisations that share their values and are committed to making a positive impact on society.

According to Deloitte's report, *A Call for Accountability and Action: The Global 2021 Millennial and Gen Z Survey*, 84% of Gen Z believes that a company's success should be measured by more than just financial performance, and 77% consider a company's social and environmental commitments when deciding where to work. Additionally, 76% of Gen Z believe that businesses have a responsibility to address social issues.

Gen Z also use social media as a tool for activism and social change. They use platforms like Twitter, Instagram and TikTok to raise awareness about social issues such as environmental sustainability to advocate for change and hold individuals and organisations accountable.

Setting objectives

Now that you're clear on your business 'why', it's time to set objectives.

Having clear objectives is important for several reasons. First, objectives provide clarity and focus. They help you define exactly what you want to achieve and outline how you will get there. They ensure that efforts and resources are directed towards the most important tasks and priorities. Objectives act as benchmarks (points of reference) and allow you to assess performance, identify areas for improvement, and make the necessary adjustments to stay on the right path.

When I studied marketing at Sheffield Hallam University, I learned the key questions outlined by Richard M.S. Wilson and Colin Gilligan in the core text, *Strategic Marketing Management: Planning, Implementation and Control*. I still have the book on my shelf, and find this five-part structure easy to remember and follow:

1. Where are we now?
2. Where do we want to be?
3. Which way is best?
4. How might we get there?
5. How can we ensure arrival?

The questions guide thinking and planning by starting with an assessment of the current situation, and then defining the destination (end goals). We can then evaluate various approaches, devise an effective way forward and implement measures to ensure we achieve what we set out to do.

Setting objectives isn't easy. Our research data indicates some uncertainty about how to determine the right objectives for social media. By 'right', we mean setting objectives that are aligned with the overall goals of the organisation and provide a clear direction for social media marketing efforts.

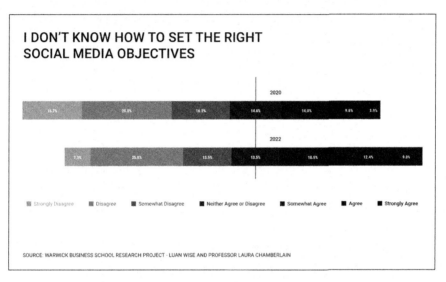

Figure 2.4. Responses to the statement, 'I don't know how to set the right social media objectives.'

In 2020, 57.9% of respondents said they knew how to set the right social media objectives; in 2022, however, this had decreased to under half (46.6%) of respondents (Figure 2.4).

In 2022, 39.9% of respondents said that they didn't know how to set the right social media objectives, an increase from 27.5% in 2020. Others stated that they were uncertain how to set the right social media objectives: 14.6% in 2020 and 13.5% in 2022.

In addition to the online questionnaire data, we explored objectives in the qualitative interviews. Below are just two responses that highlighted the lack of clear direction for social media marketing.

> I'm just putting it [social media posts] out there because I've been told to.

> With social media, we're just going through the motions without achieving anything in particular.
> We're not really taking it seriously (yet).

To set objectives, SMART is a useful framework. The acronym stands for:

- **Specific:** Objectives should be clear and specific, clearly defining what needs to be achieved. They should answer the questions of who, what, where, when, why and how.
- **Measurable:** Objectives should have quantifiable criteria that allow progress to be tracked and measured.
- **Achievable:** Objectives should be realistic and attainable. They should consider available resources, skills and constraints to ensure that they are within reach.
- **Relevant:** Objectives should be relevant and aligned with the overall business strategy. They should contribute to the big picture and make a meaningful impact.
- **Time-bound:** Objectives should have a specific time frame or deadline. This helps in creating a sense of urgency and focus, enabling effective planning and execution. It also enables you to see how many tasks you have to do. When you set your time period, ensure that you have no more than five active objectives in progress.

'Increase social media followers' is not a SMART objective. It lacks specificity, measurability and a timeframe. It does not provide any guidelines on how much the social media following should be increased by, or how it might be achieved.

A SMART objective would be to increase your Instagram followers by 20% within three months by consistently posting engaging content, using relevant hashtags and collaborating with influencers. This objective is specific (increasing Instagram followers), measurable (20% growth), achievable (through posting content and collaborations), relevant (to improve social media presence) and time-bound (within three months).

Here are two more examples that align social media marketing objectives with goals from the business plan:

- To generate 500 pre-orders for a new fashion product from young adult women aged 18-25 within the first two weeks of product launch through a combination of social media advertising, influencer collaborations, and competitions This objective is SMART because it is specific (pre-orders from young adult women aged 18-25), measurable (500 pre-orders), achievable (through targeted advertising and collaborations), relevant (aligns with the business goal of launching a new fashion product), and time-bound (within the first two weeks of product launch).
- To generate 50 qualified leads from key decision-makers in the IT industry within three months by leveraging LinkedIn advertising, content creation, and active engagement with relevant LinkedIn groups. This objective is SMART because it is specific (qualified leads from key decision-makers in the IT industry), measurable (50 leads), achievable (through LinkedIn advertising and targeted engagement), relevant (aligns with the organisation's goal of reaching decision-makers in the IT industry), and time-bound (within three months).

I spoke to Darren Knight, former-Executive Director at Cheltenham Borough Council, about the importance of setting SMART objectives when using social media. He said: *'Setting a SMART objective not*

*only gives the communications team focus but also allows us to
measure the impact of the content and engagement techniques used.'*
You can read more in the case study below.

**Case study: The use of LinkedIn by Cheltenham Borough
Council**

Before initiating a project to focus on LinkedIn, Cheltenham
Borough Council had an established but dormant LinkedIn
company Page with no posts; the communication team had little
experience using the platform.

To address this, the council set a SMART objective (to grow
the number of followers by 50 per month within three months),
and a plan to do this (by creating engaging content to promote
the council's strategic projects, attract job applicants and
complement business communications).

The Council successfully grew and engaged its LinkedIn
followers through organic activity and became an award-winning
Council and one of the top-performing Councils in the UK. Its
target of 50 followers per month was consistently exceeded (at
one point they achieved an average of 121 new followers each
month).

Showing the value of LinkedIn by reporting against objectives
allowed the communications team to get senior-level buy-in and
involvement.

They all learned from the process, adjusted their approach
along the way, and applied techniques that improved their
social media capability across other platforms. Its targeted use

---

of LinkedIn helped the council engage more effectively with the local business community, position itself as an employer of choice, and contribute to the local government sector through collaboration and sharing of best practices.

Overall, the council's approach to using LinkedIn has proved successful. It has achieved its objectives, which were measured through a combination of metrics and perception measures, as part of its wider communications and marketing performance indicator scorecard.

Follow Cheltenham Borough Council on LinkedIn at: www.linkedin.com/company/cheltenham-borough-council/

Try not to have too many objectives in play at any given time. By focusing on a select few objectives, you can allocate your resources more efficiently, closely monitor your progress, and make timely adjustments as needed to achieve your desired outcomes.

Chapter summary

This chapter has explored the importance of being intentional with social media, by aligning social media marketing goals and objectives with the overall business strategy. We have learned about the need to define a strategy before diving into tactics, and how to set SMART objectives. We've also learned the importance of understanding your why. This is all essential background work to ensure that the social media marketing plan you build for your organisation is successful and sustainable.

Actions

- Make sure you have access to your business plan so that you understand your organisation's vision, mission and 'big picture' view.
- Watch Simon Sinek's TED Talk, 'Start with Why' on YouTube. Visit www.simonsinek.com for his books – including *Start with Why* and *Find your Why* and other resources – to help find your own purpose.
- When setting objectives, ensure that you include all five SMART criteria – specific, measurable, achievable, relevant and time-bound.

Chapter 3

Defining your target audience

In this chapter, we will:

- Find out about generational differences in the use of social media.
- Explore the marketing fundamentals of market segmentation and targeting.
- Learn how to create customer personas.

As social media marketers, we must grasp a crucial reality: we are not our target audience. What we do on social media for work is not necessarily aimed at people like us. While we may be passionate about social media and have a deep understanding of how it all works, our thoughts and usage patterns are unlikely to match those of the people we want to communicate with.

To reach and engage with our target audience, we must step into their shoes and understand their preferences, motivations and behaviours. This is where personas come into play. Personas serve as a valuable tool in marketing, allowing us to create fictional representations that capture the key characteristics and needs of a group of people.

A research study by Aimia (2012) reveals six social media personas that can help us understand the differing levels of involvement and engagement by people who use social media. Although the world has changed since the research, I believe that these groupings are still relevant (and have found no more recent studies). These descriptions will help us to start thinking in the right way to create our own customer personas.

The six social media user personas are:

- **No-shows** – those who have not logged on to a social network in the past 30 days. A typical no-show exhibits a low degree of trust in social media and has no interest in broadcasting their activities or interests to anyone.
- **Newcomers** – typically, these are passive users of a single social media network. A passive user may reluctantly join Facebook, for example, in order not to feel 'left behind'. Newcomers primarily use social media to enhance their offline relationships.
- **Onlookers** – these users may lurk on several social media networks, but post infrequently. They rely on social media to keep up with the online lives of others within their social networks but are reluctant to share details about themselves.
- **Cliquers** – people who are active on a single network, such as Facebook. Most of their online sharing includes photos, status updates and comments. Within their small network of close friends and family, they're active and influential.
- **Mix-n-minglers** – the largest group of social media users, they participate actively on multiple social networking platforms. They like to follow brands in order to receive

offers and keep up with the latest news. Within their network of friends, they're influential – and they make many friends online.

- **Sparks** – the most active and deeply engaged users of social media. Sparks engage with brands frequently and will serve as enthusiastic ambassadors for their favourites.

Digital natives and digital immigrants

While Aimia's six personas categorise everyone who uses social media, when discussing social media we are often also drawn into a discussion around 'generational use' and the difference between digital natives and digital immigrants.

US author Mark Prensky coined the term 'digital native' to describe the post-millennial generation who were born in the age of digital technology. Prensky said of digital natives: 'Our students today are all "native speakers" of the digital language of computers, video games and the internet.'

Those who have experienced the pre-internet world are known as 'digital immigrants' – people who have had to learn how to communicate online. This includes boomers, Generation X and early-year millennials. Figure 3.1 shows a timeline of generations, along with an indicator of some key dates – the launch of the internet, the launch of LinkedIn, and the first iPhone.

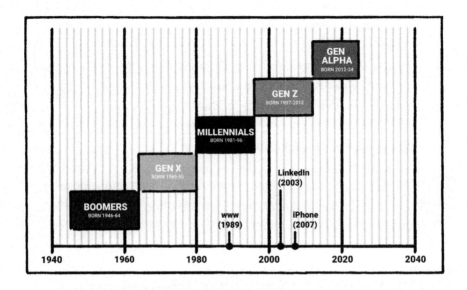

Figure 3.1. A timeline of generations.

Generational cohorts are often characterised by unique experiences and traits. Boomers, born between the mid-1940s and mid-1960s, grew up during a time of economic growth and cultural change. They tend to value hard work, loyalty, and stability. Gen X, born between the mid-1960s and 1980, experienced a shift in societal norms and witnessed the rise of technology. They are often considered independent, adaptable, and resourceful. Millennials, born between the early 1980s and mid-1990s, are the first generation to grow up with widespread access to the internet and digital technology.

As true digital natives, Gen Z, born between the mid-1990s and early 2010s are characterised by constant connectivity and access to information. They are known for their tech-savviness, entrepreneurial mindset, and social activism, with a strong desire for authenticity, inclusivity and social change.

Generation Alpha, born from 2012 onwards, will start to reach the age of 13 (the minimum age for setting up social media accounts) in 2025. They are the first generation to be entirely born in the twenty-first century, to millennial parents.

Case study: The divide between digital natives and digital immigrants

During an in-house training session for a public sector organisation, I witnessed first-hand the divide between digital natives and digital immigrants.

I was working with an established communications team. When I asked them to share their thoughts about social media for their organisation, the older members of the team focused on the technology and negative privacy-related issues that had been recently reported in the news. They showed little interest in social media as a marketing communications channel and concluded that social media was a role for a digital native, and not for them.

When the digital native in the room – an intern – stood up to explain her thoughts, she agreed that she was comfortable with the technology and how to create messages to post on social media, but she was not confident in using social media for her new role in the organisation. She had not been briefed on what to post on social media; she had just been told to 'do it'. The intern admitted she didn't understand the target audience, the messages the organisation wished to convey, and the actions it wanted customers to take after seeing its social media posts.

In response, the others in the room – an experienced communications team – knew exactly what to say and who the target audience was, and happily shared this information. The digital immigrants had allowed fears around new technology, and a new marketing channel, to become a barrier to effective communications.

Embracing the potential of social media as a powerful marketing communications channel requires a collective understanding of the target audience, key messages, and desired customer actions.

Challenging assumptions and stereotypes

The Chartered Institute of Marketing (CIM) *Impact of Marketing* report (2022) highlights that digital natives are becoming the majority population within the marketing community. We are seeing the rise of the first social media natives, and a rising sense of uncertainty among social media immigrants, who may have the preconception that younger people have better digital skills than they do.

We must not assume that everyone born before 2000 struggles to use social media, and those born after 2000 find it easy. In *Myths of Social Media (Chapter 19),* Michelle Carvill and Ian MacRae suggest that there are two major problems with the myth that digital natives are all social media experts:

1. This stereotype, like all stereotypes, is not universally true for all members of a group.
2. Personal use of social media does not necessarily translate into effective use of social media for business.

The reality I see and hear in my own work is that digital skills and social media expertise cannot be solely attributed to age or generational labels. As technology continues to evolve at a rapid pace, both digital natives and immigrants face challenges in keeping up with the latest trends and advancements. The digital skills gap affects people of all ages; a 2022 study by HP found that 20% of Gen Z feel 'tech shame' when experiencing a digital issue, compared to just 4% of workers over 40.

To navigate these challenges, it is valuable to nurture an environment for collaboration and to provide targeted support and resources (such as this book!). We'll talk more about engaging employees with social media in Chapter 6.

A clear vision of your products and services

'People don't want to buy a quarter-inch drill.
They want a quarter-inch hole.'

Theodore Levitt

What Levitt, a Harvard Business School professor, meant by the above quote is that customers are not interested in the product itself, but rather in what the products can do for them.

In other words, customers don't buy a drill for the sake of owning a drill, but because they need to make a hole of a certain size. They may wish to put up a shelf to keep their book collection in order, or to display some family photographs on a wall. This is what they are really buying.

The quote highlights the importance of customer-centricity in marketing and the need for organisations to focus on the value their products and services provide: that is, the problems they solve, rather than the product features or specifications. Your target audience does not care about the hourly output of your manufacturing equipment!

Here are some more examples:

Problem: A busy lifestyle and a lack of time to cook healthy meals.
Solution: Meal delivery services, such as HelloFresh or Gousto, deliver pre-measured ingredients and recipes to your door, making it easier and quicker for you to cook healthy meals at home.

Problem: High electricity bills and environmental concerns.
Solution: Smart home technology, such as Nest or Ecobee, that allows homeowners to control their home's energy use, save money on electricity bills, and reduce their carbon footprint.

Problem: Difficulty managing and organising work tasks.
Solution: Project management software, such as Trello or Asana, helps teams to collaborate more effectively, stay on top of deadlines, and manage their workload more efficiently.

Problem: Keeping track of finances and expenses.
Solution: A cloud-based accounting software, such as FreeAgent or Xero, that simplifies financial management, automates bookkeeping tasks and provides real-time insights into business finances.

Problem: Not enough time to maintain an active social media presence.
Solution: A social media management tool, such as Hootsuite or Sprout Social, that allows organisations to manage multiple social media accounts, schedule posts and measure results.

Do you have a clear vision of the problems you solve for your target audience?

Think about one of your products or services. Write down the problem someone would need to have before they buy it, and the solution you provide, in the space below:

Problem:

_____

_____

Solution:

_____

_____

_____

_____

Market segmentation

'Market segmentation is the process of dividing the total market for a good or service into several segments, each of which tends to be homogenous in all significant aspects with others within the segment, and heterogeneous from those in other segments.'

Professor William J. Stanton

What we've described above – the problem a customer has that is solved by your product or service – is the 'market'. However, not all customers who share a problem are the same, and a problem can be solved in a number of different ways.

A market is the total of all products and services that customers perceive as being capable of satisfying the same need or solving the same problem. For example, the home cleaning market includes all products and services that customers perceive as satisfying their need to clean their homes. This could include cleaning supplies such as washing-up liquid and sponges through to tools such as vacuum cleaners and other options such as professional cleaning services.

Segmentation refers to the process of dividing a market into smaller groups or segments. For example, the professional cleaning services market could be divided into areas such as window cleaning, or carpets and upholstery. It could also be segmented by a customer's preference for natural, organic and eco-friendly products.

There's no right or wrong way to segment a market, though it should be based on industry knowledge and data insights, and be big enough to deliver your business strategy.

Most organisations will use a variety of factors, such as the following:

- **Demographic segmentation:** Dividing the market by demographic variables, such as age, sex, income, education level and occupation.
- **Geographic segmentation:** Dividing the market by geographic region, such as country or city.
- **Psychographic segmentation:** Dividing the market by lifestyle, personality, values and attitudes.
- **Behavioural segmentation:** Dividing the market by customer behaviour, such as buying habits, product usage and brand loyalty.
- **Occasion-based segmentation:** Dividing the market based on specific occasions or events, such as holidays, festivals or seasonal changes.

- **Benefit-based segmentation:** Dividing the market based on the benefits that customers seek from a product or service.
- **Firmographic-based segmentation:** Dividing the market based on business-related characteristics such as organisation size, industry and turnover.

We can see how segmentation works in practice in the following case study.

Case study: Hilton

Hilton is a global hospitality organisation that operates several hotel brands, each targeting a specific market segment. The criteria that Hilton uses for segmentation include factors such as customer demographics, travel purposes and preferences.

Hilton's market segmentation strategy allows the organisation to offer a range of hotel brands that appeal to different customer segments, from luxury travellers to budget-conscious families. For example:

Luxury segment: The luxury segment includes brands such as Waldorf Astoria, LXR and Conrad, which target high-end travellers looking for luxury accommodations and personalised service. These hotels often have high-end facilities such as spas, fine dining restaurants and concierge services.

Full-service segment: The full-service segment includes brands such as Hilton and DoubleTree, which offer a range of facilities and services to leisure and business travellers.

These hotels often have on-site restaurants, fitness centres and meeting spaces.

- **Lifestyle segment:** The lifestyle segment includes brands such as Curio and Tapestry, which offer unique and locally inspired experiences to travellers who value authenticity and a sense of place. These hotels often have a more casual, laid-back atmosphere, with a focus on local culture and community.

- **Select-service segment:** The select-service segment includes brands such as Home2 and Homewood Suites, which offer affordable, practical accommodations to value-conscious travellers. These hotels often have fewer facilities and services than full-service hotels but provide a comfortable and convenient place to stay.

You can find out more about Hilton's hotel brands at: www.hilton.com/en/brands/

Hilton uses social media to engage with customers, promote its brands and share information about its products and services. Here are some examples of how Hilton uses social media marketing for its brands:

- **Hilton Hotels & Resorts:** Hilton Hotels & Resorts has a strong presence on social media platforms like Instagram, Facebook and Twitter. The brand uses social media to showcase its luxurious hotels and resorts, as well as to engage with customers and share information about promotions and events. For example, the Hilton Hotels & Resorts Instagram account (@hiltonhotels) features stunning photos of its properties around the world, as well as user-generated content from guests who have stayed at Hilton Hotels.

> **DoubleTree by Hilton:** DoubleTree by Hilton is known for its signature warm chocolate chip cookies, and the brand uses social media to play up this unique selling point. The DoubleTree by Hilton Instagram account (@doubletree) features mouth-watering photos of its cookies, as well as photos of its hotels and resorts.

As the Hilton case study shows, an organisation can choose to target more than one segment within a market, with different product and service offerings. This is typical; however, it does add multiple layers of complexity to marketing communications!

Selecting your target market

Once you have identified the segments within a market, you can then select which ones you wish to target, based on various factors such as size, growth potential, profitability and alignment with the business's mission and values. As renowned academic Michael E. Porter said in his 1996 'What Is Strategy?' article for *Harvard Business Review*, 'The essence of strategy is choosing what not to do.' You can't market to everyone! You need to make some choices (you can always review them and change your approach later on).

The segment or segments you select become your target market.

Once you have identified your target market, it's time to further narrow your focus to the group of people within that market who are most likely to be interested in your product or service. This is known as your target audience.

As an example, let's take an organisation that specialises in outdoor adventure gear. Their target market may be outdoor enthusiasts, but their target audience would be a more defined segment within that market, such as keen hikers and backpackers who are looking for lightweight, durable equipment for long-distance treks.

Another example could be a software development company. Their target market might be businesses in various industries seeking software solutions, but their target audience could be narrowed down to a specific segment, such as medium-sized logistics companies looking to optimise their supply chain management.

It's important to note that knowing and focusing on a target audience does not necessarily exclude those that sit outside the group from buying your product or service; it simply means that they are not where you are focusing your marketing efforts and resources.

Before we move on to the process of understanding more about your target audience, let's consider why this is relevant to social media marketing.

First, we are using social media to communicate with people. We need to understand our target audience so we can select the most appropriate social media platforms to use. With numerous options available, it can be overwhelming to choose where to invest our time and resources. But if we understand our target audience's demographic information, preferences, motivations and behaviour patterns, we can identify the social media platforms they are more likely to use and engage with. That is where we'll be focusing our efforts; on our target audience.

Second, the more details we know about who we are communicating with, the better we can tailor our content to resonate with their interests, values and desires. This understanding helps us to create engaging, relevant content that can effectively move people through the buying decision process.

The key stakeholders behind a buying decision

We must recognise that the target audience for our social media marketing activity is not always going to be the end user of the product or service; there are often other stakeholders involved in the buying decision process, and we also need to consider and create content, for them.

Particularly in B2B marketing, it is rare for a buying decision to be made by an individual. Depending on the product or service required, and how much it costs, there will most likely be a decision-making unit (DMU) involved, made up of individuals with different roles and responsibilities relating to the problem/need that they are looking to resolve. This is shown in Figure 3.2.

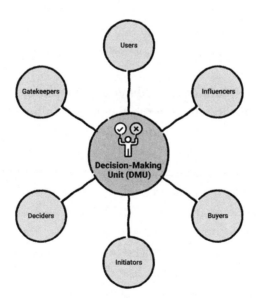

Figure 3.2. The decision-making unit (DMU).

There are several roles involved in the decision-making unit:

- **Initiators** are the people who first identify the problem/need for buying a particular product or service.
- **Buyers** are the people who have formal authority to negotiate terms of purchase with suppliers.
- **Gatekeepers** are those who control the flow of information to others. They may be asked to collect information and/or to filter what information gets through to other members of the DMU. Do not underestimate the power of the gatekeeper!
- **Users** are the people within the organisation who will use the product or service. In many cases, they may also be the initiator.
- **Influencers** are those who can influence the buying decision for a number of reasons. They may include paid advisors and consultants external to the organisation. They can also include friends and family members.
- **Deciders** are the people who have the final say in the buying decision. Deciders usually rely on advice from other members of the DMU, and are influenced strongly by gatekeepers.

Consider some recent purchases you have made, at home, and at work. Who was involved in the buying decision? What stage of the AIDA process did they engage with most?

As far as possible, all the decision-making unit roles need to be addressed by social media marketing, both in terms of deciding which platforms to use to communicate with each member of the DMU, but also in terms of the content you create and share. You might find that different members of the DMU use social media differently, and this needs to be taken into consideration as you build your customer personas and one-page social media marketing plan.

Additional resources

Those who have already studied marketing will know that the process of market segmentation and targeting is followed by a third step, positioning. While developing a full marketing strategy is outside the scope of this book, take a look at Al Ries and Jack Trout's *Positioning: The Battle for Your Mind.*

Customer personas

A customer persona, also known as a buyer persona or ideal customer portrait, is a reflection of your ideal target customer based on research and data. It is a detailed profile that includes your customer's demographic information, motivations, preferences and behaviours.

Customer personas help organisations to better understand and empathise with their target audience, allowing them to tailor their product development, customer experiences and marketing activities to meet their needs and preferences. By creating customer personas, you can make informed decisions about activities within your organisation, including social media marketing, based on a deep understanding of target audience characteristics and desires.

A customer persona is often template-led, although the questions you ask to create personas for your organisation should be tailored to your industry, products and services. Figure 3.3 shows what a customer persona template could include.

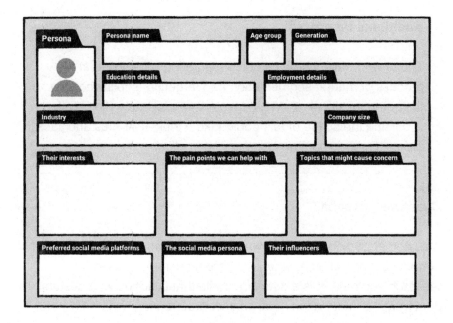

Figure 3.3. A customer persona template.

To access a free online tool to help you create a customer persona, visit www.luanwise.co.uk/books/planning-for-success/persona-generator or scan the QR code below.

There are several approaches to preparing personas. Starting with industry research and published reports is useful. In the UK, the Office for National Statistics (www.ons.gov.uk) is a good resource for reports related to the economy, population and society at national, regional and local levels. For similar data for non-UK countries, you can find resources via the United Nations statistics division (https://unstats. un.org/home/nso_sites).

Industry reports can be found via market research organisations such as Mintel (www.mintel.com) or Keynote (www.marketresearch. com). These publicly available reports often share information on market size and trends, market segmentation, competitor insights, market forecasts and more. They can be purchased online but are usually available to view via public libraries and through professional association membership services.

Combining published research such as Mintel or Keynote reports with your own business data and research is essential to help you build the best understanding of your target audience. Don't restrict your research to reading, though. Ethnography is the practice of observing people in their own environment to understand their experiences, perspectives and everyday practices, and I've used this approach on many client projects.

You should also consider speaking to existing and prospective customers one to one or via focus group interviews. Existing customers have already been through the buying decision process and can share their experiences with you, and you can dive deeper into their responses by asking additional questions.

Of course, social media can also help you build your customer personas. It's particularly useful for keeping your insights up to date, due to its real-time nature. For example, you may learn about new influencers your audience like to follow and engage with. These could become relevant future partners for you. You might also spot changes in the language that's used, or changes in the emojis used, for example. Is the tone of voice becoming more informal on a social media platform, perhaps?

As you are building your customer personas, ensure that you are following your target audience on social media. Join the groups where they hang out. Groups, for example on Facebook and LinkedIn, offer excellent opportunities to build networks and share insights as part of a community. Look for conversations and discussions related to your industry, products or services. Pay attention to the topics covered, and the problems people are discussing.

At this stage, no doubt you are asking yourself how many customer personas you will need for your organisation. The answer is that you will need to do the preparation to find the answer! By immersing yourself in industry reports and engaging with customers directly, you will gain valuable insights that will help you to identify distinct groups of individuals based on their characteristics. You are looking for similarities, not differences. Depending on the nature of your business, you may find that one or two personas suffice, or you may discover the need for ten or even more.

Giving each of your customer personas a name, such as 'Sally the Small Business Owner', adds a human touch and makes it easier to relate to your customers and empathise with their unique characteristics and needs. You can also use the names when you refer to the customer personas internally. Personas are not just useful for social media marketing so do make sure you share the information with your colleagues and external partners. Remember, social media marketing is not an isolated activity or an add-on to other marketing activity. For best results, everything needs to be fully integrated.

Finally, keep in mind that personas are not set in stone; they can, and will, evolve over time. As you gather more information you can add new personas, or merge existing ones if you find more commonalities. I recommend conducting a comprehensive review of your customer personas at least once a year to ensure they reflect the evolving characteristics of your target audience.

Additional resources

If you find this task daunting, don't worry. You should not create customer personas alone! You should involve your colleagues in the research and preparation. You can even outsource the development work to a freelancer or agency if you prefer (and have the budget available).

For more on personas, I recommend reading *Buyer Personas: How to Gain Insight Into Your Customer's Expectations, Align Your Marketing Strategies and Win More Business* by Adele Revella.

Chapter summary

In this chapter, we have recognised the need to step into the shoes of our target audience. Customer-centricity means focusing on your customers, and being guided by understanding how your product or service solves their problems. Refining the market through segmentation and creating customer personas is essential to help you get to know and understand your chosen target audience/s.

Actions

- For each of your products and services, write down the problems you solve for your customers.
- Be clear about how your market is segmented, and which audience/s your organisation is focused on targeting.
- Understand who might be involved in the buying decision process, and which roles within the decision-making unit you might need to address and prioritise for social media marketing.
- Revisit existing customer personas or start afresh using the persona generator by visiting www.luanwise.co.uk/books/ planning-for-success/persona-generator or by scanning the QR code below. There is space to include the names of your personas on the one-page social media marketing plan template.
- Follow your target audience on different social media platforms. This includes your current customers, and also potential customers.
- Which groups/communities are you currently participating in? Review the list to check that they are still relevant and useful to you. Do some research on new communities you might join. List them on your one-page social media marketing plan.

Chapter 4

Examining the social media competition

In this chapter, we will:

- Understand the role of competitor research in social media marketing planning.
- Learn the value of social media monitoring and listening.
- Decide which social media platforms are the best fit for your organisation.

Understanding who your competitors are, and what they are doing, is a vital component of successful social media marketing planning. While some organisations may prefer to focus solely on their own activities, neglecting what's happening around them can be risky. Your social media marketing content will be viewed alongside thousands of other posts, so it's valuable to understand how you sit within the context of the information your target audience is viewing.

We have already learned about the importance of understanding changes in social media; these platforms provide us with the opportunity to gather real-time insights into what other organisations in our market are doing. I believe that's too valuable (and freely available) to ignore!

By researching competitors, we can understand more about our own performance on social media: what we might be able to achieve, and how we compare to others (more on this in Chapter 7). To note, the aim of researching our competitors is to gain actionable insights for our own social media marketing activity, not to cause harm or undermine others.

We can gather insights into how other organisations are using social media to communicate information about their products and services. We can learn about their pricing models. We can learn about their people. We can learn about their customers. We can see when things are going well, and perhaps when issues are escalating. In turn, this information helps us understand how we can differentiate ourselves from our competition, to identify new opportunities, and help us make more informed decisions about our own social media marketing objectives and the content we share.

Differentiation

In *The Competitive Advantage: Creating and Sustaining Superior Performance,* Michael E. Porter wrote that strategy targets either cost leadership, market segmentation or differentiation. These are known as Porter's three generic competitive strategies and can be applied to any size or type of business.

Differentiation refers to the process of establishing a unique and compelling identity for a product, service, or brand that sets it apart from competitors in the mind of its customers. The goal of differentiation is to highlight distinct attributes or qualities that make the offering more desirable, relevant, and valuable to the target audience. By effectively differentiating themselves, organisations can create a competitive advantage and position their offerings as the preferred choice in the market.

To achieve successful differentiation, marketers identify and emphasise key points of contrast that resonate with their target audience. These differentiators can include product features, performance, quality, design, pricing, customer service, or even the brand's personality and values. By effectively communicating these unique selling points through social media and other marketing channels, organisations can shape customers' perceptions, ultimately leading to increased brand loyalty and customer retention.

For more on differentiation, take a look at *Differentiate or Die* by Jack Trout and Steve Rivkin.

Types of competitor

There are two types of competitors to consider:

1. Direct competitors: Organisations offering similar products or services and targeting the same audience.
2. Indirect competitors: Organisations targeting the same audience but offering different products or services.

Analysing social media competition starts with identifying your competitors, direct and indirect. You might do this for your organisation overall, or perhaps you need to do this based on a competitor list for individual products or services.

It's likely that you know, without thinking too hard, who your competitors are. If you're unsure, or you're considering entering a new market, then industry reports such as the previously mentioned Mintel or Keynote usually include a list of leading companies and brands in the sector.

You may also be able to find research that provides insights into indirect competitors. For example, the *UCAS Freshers Report: Student Spends and Trends 2022* (for first-year university students in the UK) lists where students prefer to buy groceries while at university (in case you were wondering, Tesco tops the list, followed jointly by Aldi and Lidl), plus their top 20 favourite brands (Amazon is number one). If I was working with an organisation with a similar target audience, I would certainly include these organisations in my social media competitor watch list.

I would also include industry bodies and professional memberships as indirect competitors, as they often have large followings with a similar target audience profile.

For example, if my target audience included UK marketing and communications professionals, I would follow social media accounts for the Chartered Institute of Marketing (CIM), the Institute of Data and Marketing (IDM), the Chartered Institute of Public Relations (CIPR) and the Public Relations and Communications Association (PRCA).

Make sure you ask about direct and indirect competitors as part of your customer persona research; take the opportunity to gather as many insights as you can. You can also look through your target audience accounts on social media to see who they are following and engaging with. The information is all out there – you just need to decide what you want to know, and go and find it!

Analysing competitors' social media presence

Once you have defined your competitor set, it's time to start analysing your competitors' social media presence. I would recommend that after an initial review is carried out, it is monitored regularly and updated annually.

Research the social media platforms your competitors are using and start to follow their accounts. You can do this via your organisation's profiles or, if you prefer, use a personal account. On Twitter, you could use a private list so that your competitor is not aware (more on Twitter Lists in Chapter 5).

A good place to start is a website, where social media links are usually included in the footer. You should also do a search on each social media platform for organisation and brand names.

Larger organisations often have multiple accounts on platforms such as Twitter and Instagram. Sometimes this is intentional – for example, a dedicated customer service account and a news account – or sometimes it happens due to a lack of communication and strategic planning between internal departments.

Once you have a list of competitor accounts, make a note of:

- Branding, including profile and header image.
- Their 'About' section/bio description.
- Website links used in bios.

The account's 'About' description or bio should indicate the purpose of a social media account. This can provide valuable insights, along with the links the organisation shares in its bio. Which website pages are they driving their social media traffic towards?

You should also look at:

- How many followers do they have?
- How often do they post content?
- What content formats are they using?
- What posts do they have pinned?
- What 'Highlight' categories are they using on Instagram?

- What hashtags are they using?
- Do they include a branded hashtag that you could follow?
- Who is engaging with their content?
- What kind of content do their audiences engage with most/ least?
- What comments do their audiences leave?
- How does the organisation respond to comments?

These are all questions you can ask when reviewing your competitors' social media presence. Decide what questions are most relevant for your organisation, and set up suitable templates – perhaps in Microsoft Excel, Google Sheets and/or PowerPoint – to capture the information. It's useful to share key insights with your colleagues, alongside your regular performance reports, or sooner if the information is timely and requires immediate action.

For data related to content – that is, frequency of posting and engagements – it's possible to gather this information directly via the platforms, or by using third-party tools such as Hootsuite (www. hootsuite.com), Sprout Social (www.sproutsocial.com), or FanPage Karma (www.fanpagekarma.com).

I like to use the Social Media Tracker from Semrush (www.semrush. com/social-media/) to access data for competitor analysis. Semrush provides audience, activity and engagement data for Facebook, Twitter, Instagram, YouTube and Pinterest. You can find a user guide for Social Tracker at www.semrush.com/kb/33-social-media-tool.

Using Facebook Insights, you can compare the performance of your business and content with similar organisations on Facebook. You can 'add a list of businesses' to see total page likes, follower growth and number of posts over a selected time period.

LinkedIn is more restrictive about providing third-party tools with access to its data. If you are a company Page administrator, you can access Competitor Analytics for Pages. You can list up to ten Pages for monitoring, and view follower numbers, number of posts and engagement data for specific date ranges.

Your competitors' advertising activity

It's also possible to learn about your competitors' paid-for activity on social media.

On LinkedIn, you can view posts on any company Page, by type. This includes images, videos, articles, documents and ads.

For Meta (Facebook and Instagram) you can access their Ad Library at https://www.facebook.com/ads/library.

The Ad Library shows all ads currently running across Meta apps and can be searched by country and keyword. An ad will appear in the Ad Library within 24 hours from the time it gets its first impression (when the ad is displayed or seen by a user). You cannot see targeting criteria or budget information. You do not need a Facebook account to access the Ad Library.

TikTok's Ad Library, part of the TikTok Creative Centre (https://ads.tiktok.com/business/creativecenter) enables you to search for the best-performing ad campaigns by industry sector and region. You can also see how trends have been used to inspire ads.

If you are following competitors on social media, it's also likely that their ads will show up in your newsfeed. Tap on the three dots on the ad (top right) and select 'why am I seeing this ad?'; you will then be shown the targeting criteria.

Even if you are not advertising on social media, it can be very useful to look at competitors' ads. You can identify the products and services they are promoting and see what creative assets they might be testing, such as variations of text, imagery and calls to action.

You will be gathering lots of data, and it will take some time to sift through it. Align what you are looking for with your own social media goals to focus on finding insights that will drive actions for your own social media marketing activities.

Social media listening

When you're ready to take competitor analysis one step beyond an initial audit, you need to tap into social media listening, which can be defined as the process of identifying and assessing what is being said about an organisation, individual, product or brand on the internet, and the issues that affect it.

Tools for social media listening vary from one-off advanced searching for keywords (and hashtags) on social media platforms to sophisticated monitoring tools such as Brandwatch (www.brandwatch.com) or Talkwalker (www.talkwalker.com). Other options include Google Alerts and Twitter lists. We'll take a look at these in Chapter 5.

Social media listening within groups, such as on Facebook and LinkedIn, is a highly valuable way to gain insights into your target audience's preferences, interests, and sentiments. By actively joining and participating in relevant groups you can monitor and review discussions, comments, and feedback from potential customers; especially useful if they are mentioning the areas you specialise in. Active involvement within groups also fosters a sense of authenticity and credibility. Responding to queries, addressing concerns and engaging in meaningful conversations can help position you and your organisation as subject matter experts and a preferred solution when looking for a new supplier or partner.

Stephen Rappaport, author of *Listen First! Turning Social Media Conversations into Business Advantage* (2011), highlights two types of listening, each of which has a unique purpose:

- **Social monitoring:** Tracking online brand mentions for PR monitoring, brand tracking and customer engagement.
- **Social research:** Analysing naturally occurring online categories of conversation to better understand why people do what they do, the role brands play in their lives, and the product, branding and communications implications for brand owners.

Social monitoring is often used to identify existing conversations that require a response. Social research is more proactive and immersive. By integrating both approaches, organisations can leverage the real-time power of social media to respond to mentions as well as identify emerging opportunities.

The ContentCal case study is an excellent example of using social media listening for both monitoring and research.

Case study: ContentCal. Leveraging competitor listening for business growth

Shared by Andy Lambert, founding team and director of growth, ContentCal (sold to Adobe in 2021).

At ContentCal, we recognised the importance of competitor listening in driving our business development efforts. By monitoring conversations and engaging with disgruntled

---

customers of our key competitors, we were able to capitalise on their dissatisfaction and offer them an alternative solution. This approach played a crucial role in our business growth and success.

We trained our sales team to utilise tools like TweetDeck and Google Alerts. Every morning, for half an hour our sales representatives monitored discussions related to key phrases, competitor product names, and our competitors' social media customer support accounts.

The approach we adopted was rooted in empathy, putting power in the hands of the customer, and providing helpful solutions rather than aggressive selling tactics. We began by engaging with social media posts from unhappy users of our competitors' products by sharing a supportive comment or perhaps a funny GIF. This allowed us to establish a connection and show that we understood their frustration. We would then follow up with a direct email, offering assistance and providing resources such as a blog post or an invite to a future webinar, where appropriate. By adopting a human approach, understanding customer pain points and providing valuable resources, we built a positive sentiment around our brand, and that's probably the thing I'm most proud of.

We also leveraged social media listening to find out news about our competitors and create targeted campaigns. For example, when there was news of a price increase by a competitor, we responded with content that highlighted our competitive pricing and value. We launched a paid search campaign to capture those searching for alternative social media management tools.

Finally, we used social media listening to identify influencers who were talking about our competitors. We built relationships with them so we could get them talking about ContentCal. Over time, the people we worked with contributed the most to our reach metrics.

This is real 'in the weeds' social media activity. It's not glamorous – but it really works.

How to choose the right social media platforms for your organisation

We have now discussed the ever-changing social media landscape, set meaningful social media goals and SMART objectives, defined our target audience, and analysed our competitors. We are finally ready to choose which social media platforms to use.

To help you make this decision, ask these questions:

What do you want to achieve?

Set social media goals and objectives that align with your business plan. If your goal is to showcase visual content and reach a younger audience, platforms like Instagram or TikTok could be a good fit, due to their emphasis on visual storytelling. If website traffic is important, Instagram will not be a good fit as the option to include links is limited to your bio. Look for platforms that offer the features that align with your goals and objectives.

Who is your target audience? What social media platforms are they using?

Understanding your target audience is essential for effective platform selection. Use industry insights and customer personas to identify the social media platforms where your target audience spends the most time. For instance, if your audience consists mainly of professionals and business leaders, LinkedIn might be the ideal platform to reach them. If you want to showcase your products to Generation Z, Instagram might be the best fit.

If you have identified multiple target audiences you might need to answer this question, and the following competitor question, for each audience to guide your decision.

Ideally, you need to go to your customers. It is much harder to get your customers to come to you.

Which platforms are your competitors using? How do they use them?

If your competitors are active and successfully engaging with their audience on platforms like Facebook or Twitter, it could indicate that these platforms are a good fit for your organisation as well. If your competitors have a minimal presence or low engagement on a platform, it may suggest that it's not a suitable option for you; however, it could also mean that you could have an early adopter advantage. Will you conform to industry norms, or dare to take a risk and do something different?

What resources do you have available?

Consider the resources you have available to manage your social media presence. Different platforms require varying levels of time, effort and expertise. Evaluate your team's capabilities, budget and available tools. If, for example, you have limited resources and struggle to produce high-quality visual content and video, TikTok may not be the best fit. Instead, focusing on platforms like Twitter or LinkedIn, which involve more text-based content, could be a more suitable option (in the short term). If you don't believe you can achieve your social media goals and objectives with your existing resources, you may need to build a business case to obtain what you need for long-term success.

It's important to note that choosing the right social media platforms is not about being present or active on every single platform. Instead, it's about focusing your efforts on the platforms that align with your goals, target audience and available resources. You need to immerse yourself in social media to truly understand how they work, and what the best fit is for your organisation. You would not promote your brand on a radio station if you never listened to the radio, so please don't think you can avoid social media. You also need to get into the habit of using social media regularly to achieve your organisational goals – and this might be different to how you use social media personally.

By strategically selecting the most relevant platforms, you can maximise your impact and achieve your social media marketing goals. You can also add a new platform later, and if things change you might decide to stop using a particular platform. Before you do this, ask yourself the same set of questions:

- What do you want to achieve?
- Who is your target audience? What social media platforms are they using?
- What platforms are your competitors using? How do they use them?
- What resources do you have available?

Case study: Using social media to gather insights

You don't always have to be actively sharing content on a social media platform to find it valuable.

Penny Eccles, former-marketing director at Nottingham Trent University, shared with me a brilliant example of using social media as an onlooker. She and other board colleagues had been asked to summarise a significant industry research report over a weekend, in preparation for the Monday morning board meeting. She knew that providing an executive summary alone would not suffice.

She saw that LinkedIn and Twitter were both buzzing with conversations about the industry report, among competitors and sector policy commentators. Diving deeper, she was able to find out not just facts about the report, but also opinions, insights and a rich variety of perspectives. Competitors and mission groups were lobbying to offer their own interpretations based on the research findings, journalists were sharing their reviews in published articles, and industry commentators were engaging in thought-provoking debates about how that policy could change the higher education sector for the future.

Armed with this newfound knowledge, she crafted her response for the board and felt able to show a future-focused perspective on the nuances of the report. By incorporating real-time insights from key industry players over the space of a weekend, she provided a holistic understanding of the research findings and their potential impact on the market.

Chapter summary

In this chapter, we have explored the role of competitor research, and the need to identify direct and indirect competitors. We've looked at what questions to consider when reviewing competitors' social media accounts. We have also learned about social media listening for ongoing monitoring and research.

The information in this chapter, along with previous chapters, can guide you to make an informed decision about the right social media platforms to use for your organisation.

Actions

- List your direct and indirect competitors.
- Create a list of the social media platforms they are using, and their account details.
- Start to follow your competitors, either via your own organisation accounts, or a personal account.
- Set up a template document, perhaps in Microsoft Excel and/or Powerpoint to capture relevant competitor insights.
- Use the following questions to review your competitors' accounts. Add any additional questions relevant to your own organisation, products and services.
  - How many followers do they have?
  - How often do they post content?
  - What content formats are they using?
  - What posts do they have pinned?
  - What 'Highlight' categories are they using on Instagram?
  - What hashtags are they using?
  - Do they include a branded hashtag that you could follow?

- Who is engaging with their content?
- What kind of content do their audiences engage with most/least?
- What comments do their audiences leave?
- How does the organisation respond to comments?
- Look at your competitors' advertising activity. Note what products and services they are promoting and what creative options they might be testing.
- Review potential tools for social monitoring and identify relevant keywords and topics that you could track. Possible tools include Google Alerts, Twitter Lists, Brandwatch and Talkwalker.
- Search for relevant groups, for example on Facebook and LinkedIn, where you can engage in social research and helpful conversations with your target audiences.
- Make an informed decision about the social media platforms you will start using for your organisation by asking:
  - What do you want to achieve?
  - Who is your target audience? What social media platforms are they using?
  - What platforms are your competitors using? How do they use them?
  - What resources do you have available?
- Ensure you have internal processes in place to share competitor and audience insights with your colleagues and relevant external partners (eg agencies/freelancers).

Chapter 5

Creating a social media content calendar

In this chapter, we will:

- Learn the role of 'content pillars' and how to establish them.
- Learn about different types of content for social media, including evergreen and timely topics.
- Discover how to curate content and share content that isn't yours.

In January 1996, Bill Gates, the co-founder of Microsoft, wrote an influential essay titled 'Content is King'. In this essay, Gates accurately predicted the significance of content in the digital era, particularly on the internet. At this point, the internet was only six years old.

Gates recognised that the internet presented a new frontier for the distribution and consumption of information, entertainment and other forms of content. He emphasised that the ability to create high-quality, compelling content would be a driving force behind the success of businesses and individuals operating in this new digital world.

Over the years, Gates' prediction has proven to be remarkably accurate, particularly in the context of social media. Social media platforms have become content-driven ecosystems, where engaging and shareable content are at the heart of user interactions.

In the context of social media, 'content' refers to any type of information or media that is created and shared on social media accounts (your own, or in the form of comments on other user accounts). It serves multiple purposes, such as:

- **Informing and educating.** Content can be used to provide information and educate an audience about a specific topic, or share insights and knowledge related to a brand, product, service or industry. This can position you and your organisation as a trusted source of expertise.
- **Entertainment.** Entertaining content helps capture the attention of social media users. It can provide enjoyment, amusement or a sense of escapism for your audience.
- **Building brand identity.** Content allows organisations and individuals to showcase their unique personality, values and purpose.
- **Creating connections and starting conversations.** Content gives social media users a reason to connect with other users: people engage with content that resonates with them. This could be an initial following on Instagram, a connection request on LinkedIn, or content that sparks a conversation at any time in the relationship.

Personal branding and thought leadership

Personal branding refers to the process of establishing and promoting an individual as a brand. By positioning themselves as subject matter experts and thought leaders, individuals can leverage their personal brand to enhance their professional

---

reputation, attract opportunities, and connect with their followers and connections on a deeper level.

Richard Branson, the iconic entrepreneur and founder of Virgin Group, is a prime example of the power of personal branding. With a strong presence on social media platforms, Branson has amassed a significant following that surpasses the follower count of his brands. At the time of writing, he has 18.7 million followers on LinkedIn; Virgin Group has 274,000.

Another notable example is Victoria Beckham, the fashion designer and former Spice Girl. Beckham has successfully built a personal brand on social media that transcends her brand as a fashion designer. With a massive following on platforms like Instagram, she shares glimpses into her personal life, fashion choices, and charity work. At the time of writing, @victoriabeckham has 31.1 million followers on Instagram; @victoriabeckhambeauty has 835,000 Instagram followers.

Richard Branson and Victoria Beckham are both extremely well-known, however, I regularly see similar patterns in followers between personal accounts and corporate accounts on social media. People do business with people they know, like and trust.

In *The Social CEO: How Social Media Can Make You A Stronger Leader,* Damian Corbet shares useful case studies highlighting the opportunities for business leaders to 'get social', and the expectations we have to see leaders communicating authentically as individuals on social media.

If you're struggling to get your leadership team involved with social media I highly recommend sharing a copy of this book with them.

At Aston University in Birmingham, UK, personal branding on social media is included as part of its MBA induction sessions. I'm proud to deliver this social media training and enjoy the interactive discussions we have about the opportunities it presents.

Aimee Postle, Team Coach, Aston Centre for Enterprise, Coaching and Innovation, at Aston University says: *We operate in an increasingly connected world in which our online presence is just as important as the impact we make face-to-face. For Aston University MBA students, that means understanding how to engage effectively on professional global business platforms and how to develop their personal brand to support their future employment prospects and network expansion. Knowing how to connect and engage online makes a tangible impact on their future success.*

I recognise that the concept of personal branding can be tricky to balance.

I asked Joe Glover, Co-Founder of The Marketing Meetup, "How do you get a balance between your own personal brand, and The Marketing MeetUp brand when you post on social media?" Joe said, *"My [personal] brand is inevitably linked with The Marketing MeetUp, but I do feel like I can retain an element of personal opinion, which can sit separately from The Marketing MeetUp. Something that is difficult, especially as follower numbers have grown, is interpretation. For example, when I'm posting from me [my personal LinkedIn profile], someone may perceive that post to be The Marketing MeetUps opinion. People inevitably interpret content from their own context. The intention is to separate my own content from The MarketingMeetUp, but whether or not it's received that way, I don't know."*

Thought leadership is a crucial aspect of personal branding that deserves attention. Thought leadership refers to the practice of sharing innovative ideas, insights, and expertise within a specific industry or field. It involves establishing oneself as an authority and a trusted source of knowledge, contributing to industry discussions, and shaping the direction of conversations. Thought leaders often publish articles, speak at conferences, and engage with their audience through various channels, such as blogs and social media platforms. By actively participating in thought leadership activities, individuals can gain recognition, build credibility, and attract a loyal following, ultimately enhancing their personal brand and opening doors to new opportunities.

Like all elements of social media marketing, personal branding and thought leadership requires careful consideration, planning and measurement. If you want to learn how to develop your personal brand, *Personal Branding for Dummies* by Susan Chritton is a useful step-by-step guide.

The opportunities available through social media content, for both organisations and individuals, sound amazing, but producing good content can also be challenging.

In our own research, we found that almost half of our respondents agreed that they 'don't know what to say on social media that will be effective' (Figure 5.1). In 2020 46% of respondents were unsure about this or agreed with it; in 2022 this had increased to 47.7%.

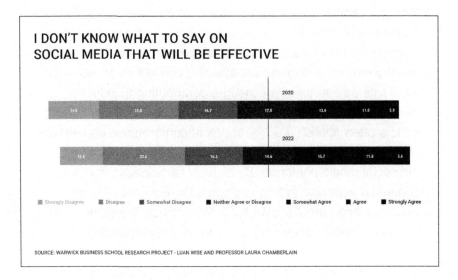

Figure 5.1. Responses to the statement, 'I don't know what to say on social media that will be effective.'

We will be looking at this challenge throughout this chapter, and how to address it using content pillars.

When managing social media on behalf of an organisation, sometimes 'not knowing what to say' on social media stems from not being the subject matter expert. The following case study has some top advice for what you can do in this situation.

Case study: Involving subject matter experts in content creation Shared by Helen Christopher, Global Marketing Director.

I've encountered the challenge of creating compelling content for social media without being a subject matter expert multiple times in my career. This struggle is particularly prevalent in industries like professional services or manufacturing, where all the specialist knowledge and technical jargon can feel overwhelming. However, I firmly believe that as marketers, our primary expertise lies in effective communications and collaboration.

Let's begin by acknowledging that we shouldn't expect subject matter experts to write the content themselves. They have their own areas of expertise; they may not possess the skill of creating engaging social media content. Instead, it's up to us to take the initiative and clearly explain to the subject matter expert what we require, and why. By articulating the purpose and goals of our social media content, we help them understand the value it brings to our organisation, and to our target audience.

If we work closely with subject matter experts, we can tap into their wealth of knowledge and insights while leveraging our marketing expertise to craft content that resonates with our target audience. Regular brainstorming sessions, interviews and discussions provide invaluable insights and help us to identify the most relevant, compelling aspects to highlight. Actively involving subject matter experts in the content creation process ensures that our content is accurate, and gives them a sense of ownership and pride in their contributions.

It's important to continue working with subject matter experts when sharing content. Authenticity and building individual networks hold immense power: I consistently advocate training for colleagues on optimising their own LinkedIn profiles and how to engage in social selling. By equipping colleagues with the necessary skills and knowledge, we empower them to amplify the reach and impact of our content while establishing themselves as thought leaders in their respective fields.

Ideas before format

Content for social media will inevitably include a mix of content created solely for use on social media, plus content that drives an audience to other resources, such as your blog or website.

As a standalone form of content, social media can involve text, plus visuals (photos and graphics), video and audio formats. For example, Instagram posts will be visual, supported by a caption. A LinkedIn or Facebook post might involve more text and be supported by an image or video. Twitter Spaces (live audio events) are promoted using text-based notifications.

All too often social media content is driven by the desire to use a specific content format rather than looking at the message that needs to be communicated. I'm sure you've had similar conversations at work about 'doing more video!' In an environment where new content formats are regularly introduced and trends are constantly evolving, I recommend focusing on developing the core idea first and then adapting it to the most suitable content format/s.

The *Content Benchmarks Report* (Sprout Social, 2023) collected and analysed data from 729,000 public social media profiles to understand what type of content people prefer (indicated by engagement metrics). Short-form video comes out top with two-thirds of consumers finding it engaging (66%), closely followed by static images (61%).

When using data to identify trends and best practices, it is important to recognise that you will need to test and measure the performance of your own content to ensure it helps you meet your business strategy and encourages your target audience to take action. Industry reports are hugely valuable, but you will find the best answer to 'what works best for you' through data and insights from your own social media accounts. Chapter 7 will help you understand the social media measurements that matter.

When social media serves as a distribution channel for other marketing content a social media post could be used to introduce a blog topic and include a website link to take people through to a website where they can read the full article. Similarly, a social media post could announce an event, and a website link can take people through to a registration page so they can add their details and attend the event. Teaser clips, behind-the-scenes footage and guest highlights can all be shared in social media posts to drive people towards a podcast.

There are so many options, and changes occur regularly. But you will need to bear in mind the resources you have available for content creation: for example, video content can take a long time to produce and may require specialist software for editing (such as Adobe Premiere Pro).

A note about organic and paid social media

Organic and paid social media are two distinct (and also complementary) approaches to using social media platforms for marketing purposes.

Organic social media refers to content and interactions that occur on social media platforms without any paid promotion. By contrast, paid social media involves investing money to promote content and reach a wider audience. It includes various advertising formats such as sponsored posts, display ads, and influencer collaborations.

Facebook began to place ads on its platform as early as 2006. Twitter enabled ads in 2010. LinkedIn, Instagram, TikTok and Snapchat all have forms of advertising available.

It is generally best to focus on getting organic content working well before investing in advertising. Building a solid foundation of organic content allows you to establish a genuine connection with your audience and gain insights into their preferences. Once you have a strong organic presence and a deep understanding of your audience, you can strategically complement your organic efforts with paid advertising to amplify your reach, target specific segments, and drive conversions.

Each social media platform that offers advertising opportunities has self-serve tools to help you set up advertising campaigns. You can learn how to do this yourself through online resources such as Meta Blueprint (https://www.facebookblueprint.com/), LinkedIn Marketing Labs (https://training.marketing.linkedin. com/) or TikTok Academy (https://my.academywithtiktok.com/ learn), or you might like to consider outsourcing if you lack the time, expertise or resources to do it effectively.

The importance of storytelling

'Marketing is no longer about the stuff you sell,
but about the stories you tell.'

Seth Godin

From prehistoric cave paintings to big-budget Hollywood movies, the desire to tell and hear stories is deeply rooted in the human experience. Storytelling is a timeless tradition that has served multiple purposes throughout history. It has been a means of preserving cultural heritage, passing down knowledge from one generation to the next, and providing entertainment.

Stories have a unique ability to capture our attention. Unlike isolated facts or information, a narrative provides context, meaning and relatability, making it easier for us to remember and connect with the content on a deeper level. If I asked you how many active Facebook users there are, would you recall the number (2.9 billion) or the comparison to countries (larger than the population of China and India combined)?

Every organisation has a wealth of stories to tell, whether about its founder's journey, the challenges it has overcome, customer success stories, or the impact it has made in the community.
As individuals, we each have our own professional story to share too. In a crowded, competitive marketplace, the ability to differentiate yourself, stand out from the crowd and be remembered is essential. By telling our unique professional story, we establish our identity, showcase our expertise, and build our credibility.

Case study: Airbnb's storytelling through social media

Airbnb is a leading global online marketplace that revolutionised the hospitality and travel industry. Founded in 2008, the company connects travellers with unique accommodations and experiences offered by individual hosts worldwide.

Airbnb excels in storytelling through social media: across multiple platforms it shares high-quality visuals, videos and user-generated content, shining a spotlight on extraordinary locations such as treehouses, castles and off-the-grid retreats.

Airbnb no longer tells its origin story about starting with a couple of broke students and an air mattress. It does not tell the story of a tech company. The idea at the core of the company is 'belonging', and this is central to Airbnb's current brand storytelling.

Airbnb understands the value of immersing yourself in local communities and cultures. By sharing narratives, vibrant photography and interviews with hosts and guests, Airbnb fosters a sense of connection and understanding. Through its storytelling, Airbnb encourages travellers to go beyond being tourists to become active participants in the local culture, embracing authentic experiences.

Follow Airbnb on social media: @airbnb

For further information on the history of Airbnb, I recommend reading *The Airbnb Story* by Leigh Gallagher, which provides an in-depth exploration of the transformative effect Airbnb had on the travel industry.

Let's explore the concept of content pillars as our foundations for storytelling.

What are content pillars?

Content pillars are the core themes or topics that guide content for an organisation or individual. They are the foundation on which all content is created and organised, and they help ensure that the content produced is aligned with the overall goals and values of the brand or individual.

Content pillars are typically determined by understanding the target audience, business strategy and industry trends. The pillars should be broad enough to allow for a variety of content types and formats, but specific enough to provide a clear direction for the content you will post and share.

If you don't have content pillars, you risk producing content that lacks direction and consistency. Without content pillars, you might find yourself creating content on an ad hoc basis, which can lead to a disjointed mix of content that doesn't align with your 'why' or objectives. This can make it difficult for your audience to understand what your brand is all about. In turn, they will be less likely to engage with your content or progress to buying your products or services. There's nothing worse than a social media account that posts so many random things that viewers forget who they are and what they do.

Content pillars are key messages that serve as headlines, guiding your content creation and sharing process. These key messages typically remain unchanged over time, unless there is a significant shift in the direction of the business or personal brand.

By consistently creating and sharing content that is in line with your content pillars, your audience will know what you do and how you can help them. They'll recognise your areas of expertise, trust you, and come to you when they need you. They may also refer you to others.

Establishing your content pillars

I recommend establishing three to five content pillars as part of your social media marketing plan. As social media does not work in a silo, the pillars should also be used across all your marketing communications, including email, print, etc.

To find your content pillars, I suggest that you start with your industry, your community, any causes you support, and what else matters to your audience. These are broad headings, and it's likely that you will refine and add to these as you start to explore them for your own organisation and/or personal brand.

- **Your industry**

  What is going on in your industry or profession? What stories might your audience already be hearing that you can share, to demonstrate that you are keeping up to date with the latest news and events?

  For example, if you are an estate agent, what's going on in the property market as a whole? If you're in recruitment, can you share information about the latest salary survey? If you're an accountant, can you share the impact of government budgets and policies?

- **Your community**

  Very often organisations play a key role in their own communities. For example, The Marketing Meetup (https://themarketingmeetup.com/) is a marketing community created by marketers, for marketers.

  Organisations that have a local workforce also have a role to play in helping the economic growth of an area, and they might be able to support other local organisations, via collaborations or partnerships.

  What communities are you a part of? What communities could you seek out and get involved with? This can reap many rewards for your organisation (not just for the purposes of creating social media content!).

- **Causes you support**

  Sharing content about the causes you support is another strong content pillar idea; many organisations and individuals have a nominated charity or provide support for specific causes.

  If you want to make a difference in the fight against digital poverty, for example, you could donate computer equipment, sponsor community-based programmes or provide free digital skills training workshops.

  Perhaps you have achieved or are working towards B Corp Certification (a designation awarded to organisations that meet very high standards in social and environmental performance, transparency, and accountability).

  Whatever causes you and your organisation support, let your followers know about it!

  It's important to tell your followers about your 'why' – it's not just your products and services they're interested in when they do business with you. Show how your values run through the heart of everything you do.

- **What matters to your audience?**

  When you post and share content on social media, it's essential to consider your target audience and hit the 'relevance' sweet spot between what you want to say and what they are interested in (Figure 5.2).

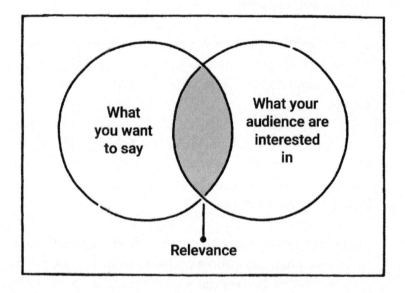

Figure 5.2. The 'relevance' sweet spot.

Content that demonstrates you understand your audience and their pain points is hugely powerful. Hopefully, you will have gathered this information as part of your customer persona preparation. This is where you can talk about the problems your products/services solve, and build trust.

For example, a virtual assistant could share content about ways to increase productivity (one of which will, no doubt, include delegating/ outsourcing work to a VA!), appealing to business owners who are struggling to find time to do everything they need to do. A career coach could provide tips for job searching, interview preparation or CV writing. They could also share content that addresses workplace challenges, such as employers that offer solutions for a better work–life balance, like flexible working practices.

Your content pillars act as a checklist for every piece of content you create and share, and every communication opportunity that arises. If it doesn't fit within your pillars, then don't pursue it. You'll confuse yourself, and your audience.

For example, one December I received a phone call from a journalist asking if I would like to offer an expert commentary on the latest John Lewis Christmas ad campaign. As much as I would have loved to have my name in a national press article, I declined the opportunity. Why? Because it didn't fit with my key messages. I'm not an expert on retail marketing, and my personal values are about positivity rather than sharing negative commentary.

Navigating vulnerability on social media

Where social media requires more personal content, finding the right balance between sharing information about yourself, so others can get to know you, and avoiding oversharing can be tricky. There is no right and wrong. This is a personal decision; but an important one.

To achieve a healthy balance, consider a few key factors. First, take the time to reflect on your personal boundaries and values. Think about what aspects of your life you feel comfortable sharing and what should remain private.

Second, practise intentionality when you post on social media. Pause and reflect before sharing personal information. Ask yourself why you want to share a particular post, and what impact it may have on yourself and others. Consider

---

the potential consequences, both positive and negative, and evaluate whether the benefits outweigh the risks. What do people need to know to do business with you and your organisation?

Last, be mindful of the digital footprint you create. Recognise that once information is shared online, it can be hard to control its spread or to erase it. Take steps to protect your privacy by adjusting your privacy settings and carefully choosing who to share personal information with.

Creating a content calendar

Now you have the pillars for your social media marketing content, you need to prepare a calendar for posting. This is a plan of your upcoming posts, organised by date.

First, consider your resources. Whenever I talk to marketers about social media, the phrase 'could be doing more' is always mentioned. We could always do more – with more time, more budget and so on – but quality (and focus) is far more important than quantity. Your content calendar needs to be achievable with the resources you have available.

Next, decide how often you will post content on your social media accounts. A quick online search will reveal many recommendations on how often to post, but you will not find a single definitive answer. Again, you need to consider what will work best for you, with the resources you have available. It is, however, useful to recognise that each social media platform operates at a slightly different pace. For example, if you were to only tweet once a day, your Tweet would quickly get lost. If you have chosen to use Twitter, you will need to plan for a higher frequency of posts, perhaps three or four per day.

Alternatively, if you have chosen LinkedIn, you can plan for much fewer posts. In my experience, a LinkedIn post continues to be visible in newsfeeds and receive engagement, for up to two weeks.

You can also take guidance from your competitor analysis to see what volume and frequency of posting is most common in your industry sector. Ultimately, you will need to test what works best for you and you will find the answer to that question in your own data (you'll discover how to do this in Chapter 7).

Once you have decided on the number of posts you will need, begin to prepare your content calendar, starting with a long-term view e.g. twelve months.

A content calendar can be as simple or as complex as you need it to be. You could use an Excel spreadsheet, online planning tools such as Asana (www.asana.com), Trello (www.trello.com) or Monday.com (www.monday.com), or the calendar feature in a social media management tool such as Hootsuite or Sprout Social.

A quick win is to add any key dates within your industry sector or events on your own business calendar that you can align social media content with.

After you have a long-term view, you can start to create more detailed plans for shorter periods, such as monthly or weekly content calendars. Planning allows you to separate 'thinking' from 'doing' and helps you maintain focus on your overall objectives. Allow for flexibility by leaving space for breaking news and trends in your calendar, and don't worry if you create more, or fewer, posts than you originally plan – number of posts should not be an objective.

Using your content pillars and broadly following a 'rule of thirds' over a month will help ensure you have a good mix that works for both your organisation and your target audience.

The three areas are:

1. **Self-promotion:** showcase your achievements (for example, key business milestones, positive reviews or awards won).
2. **Letting us get to know you:** tell us what you're doing and what you're thinking about. You could share events you're attending, behind-the-scenes stories, or challenges you've encountered.
3. **Recommendations:** share 'how to' articles, industry research, books you recommend, TED Talks to watch, etc. Recommending content that's not your own is key – we don't need to *create* all the content that we share. We'll look at curation (sharing other people's content) later in this chapter.

Figure 5.3 shows what a month on social media might look like for my marketing consultancy and training business. My content pillars focus on marketing and my specialist area of social media for business. In terms of community support, I share content for fellow marketers, fellow freelancers and also organisations within my region (South West, UK).

My social media marketing plan currently includes posting on LinkedIn, Facebook, Twitter, Instagram and TikTok. I regularly Tweet industry news, except on a Monday, when I share a round-up email newsletter. I regularly post content about business events – topics that I know matter to my audience/s. To ensure I have a mix of content (following the 'rule of thirds'), I curate and share content from others, and go 'behind the scenes' to share my love of reading and trips away in my campervan. I focus on showing up consistently.

Once I've created a monthly outline, I'll go into more detail creating the individual posts. I usually do this on a weekly basis. In my diary I also schedule time each day for reading my newsfeeds, responding to messages, and engaging with the users I follow – on profiles, pages and within groups/communities. Remember, social media is not just about creating and posting content; spending time on community management is essential to success.

Monday	Tuesday	Wednesday	Thursday	Friday	Saturday	Sunday
		1 (in)(f)(♪)(◎) Coming up this month (🐦) News	**2** (🐦) News	**3** (◎) Drinking coffee at... (🐦) News	**4**	**5**
6 (in) What I'm working on (🐦) News	**7** (in) Content share eg TedTalk (🐦) News	**8** (🐦) News	**9** (🐦) News (🐦) Event promo	**10** (◎) Event picture (f) Event picture (🐦) Event picture (🐦) News	**11** (♪)(◎) #vanlife	**12**
13 (in)(f)(◎)(🐦) Email newsletter promo	**14** (in) Collab share (f) Collab share (🐦) News	**15** (🐦) News	**16** (🐦) News	**17** (in) Key date (◎) Key date (f) Key date (🐦) News	**18**	**19**
20 (◎) Great meeting with...	**21** (in) Content promo (f) Content promo (🐦) News	**22** (🐦) News	**23** (🐦) News	**24** (🐦) News	**25** (♪)(◎) #vanlife	**26**
27 (◎) Book recommendation	**28** (in) Industry news share (🐦) News	**29** (🐦) News	**30** (🐦) News			

Figure 5.3. An example monthly social media content calendar.

105

We're stuck in a moment of not enough content versus too much.

This comment (above) from our qualitative research interviews led to an interesting discussion. Often the biggest fear is not 'knowing what to post', however, I have also seen situations where anything and everything was being shared on social media. The key, in my opinion, is to ensure consistency in visibility and that content aligns with goals and objectives. If it's relevant to your audience and fits with content pillars, then it's good to post.

Evergreen content

Evergreen content refers to content that remains relevant and valuable to audiences over an extended period. It's named after evergreen trees, which retain their leaves all year round. Unlike timely or time-sensitive content, evergreen content is not tied to specific events, trends or current news.

Evergreen content is designed to provide lasting value, and can be shared repeatedly without losing its relevance. It's OK to repeat content: you should post evergreen messages regularly, especially as you will always have potential customers coming into your marketing funnel.

After you've put the time in to plan and create evergreen content, you don't want it to be a one-hit-wonder. The lifespan of any post on social media is short (especially on Twitter). Ensure you include evergreen content when preparing your social media content calendars.

You should have evergreen content relevant for each stage of the marketing funnel: for awareness, interest, desire, action, plus loyalty and advocacy. For example, case studies and answers to your frequently asked questions (FAQs) make great evergreen content.

Do you have a content inventory?

It's useful to keep a working document of the evergreen content you have within your business, such as blogs, infographics and videos, so that you can share them regularly on social media. I suggest an Excel spreadsheet or Google Sheet with columns with the following headings

- Title
- Location (e.g. Dropbox folder or website URL)
- Customer persona (who is it for)
- Content type (e.g. video, infographic)
- Stage of the marketing funnel (e.g. awareness, interest, desire, action,
- loyalty & advocacy)
- Notes (e.g. who owns the content, when will it need updating).

This is not a quick task, although you may be able to use a plugin to export some of the information from your website. It is, however, worth the time investment as you may find valuable content that you had forgotten about.

Once you have populated your spreadsheet, can you identify content that is no longer a fit for your content pillars? Does any content need updating, or should you archive it? Use the notes column for any actions. Then you can look for gaps to fill with new content.

Repurposing content

In addition to repeating content, most evergreen content produced by your organisation can also be repurposed into different formats for sharing across social media platforms. For example, from the key headlines in a research report, you could create an infographic, which you can post on Twitter and Facebook, with a link to a website landing page (for users to download the full report).

Additional resources

Amy Woods is the CEO and founder of Content 10×, a creative agency specialising in content repurposing. I recommend reading Amy's book *Content 10×: More Content, Less Time, Maximum Results* and subscribing to her email updates via www.content10x.com.

Timely topics and trending content

One of the key benefits of social media as a marketing communications channel is its real-time nature. Some timely content can be part of your plan – you know when it is going to happen. Other content opportunities may appear on the news, while others may simply be popular and most-talked-about subjects at a particular time.

Google Trends (https://trends.google.com) and Exploding Topics (https://explodingtopics.com) are useful websites for researching trends.

Trending topics are usually displayed prominently on social media platform home pages, and these can provide opportunities for you and your organisation to join relevant conversations and engage with your audience. The speed at which topics trend can make it challenging to keep up: it's not essential to get involved with every trend, but it is useful to know what people are talking about.

When deciding whether to get involved, check your content pillars. Consider how you can ensure relevance to your audience/s. If there's not a clear fit – watch the trend for your own interest, and move on. If you've missed the moment, then don't worry – there will always be another trend to get involved with.

Having an understanding of popular culture and the current news agenda might impact your content plan even if you don't get directly involved with these topics; for example, early in the Covid-19 crisis many businesses changed their social media content plans to take into consideration the requirement to stay at home during national lockdowns, and to show empathy towards the shared concerns of their audience.

Awareness days

Awareness days, weeks or months are set up by individuals and organisations to mark an occasion or to raise money for a charity/ cause. There's an awareness day for just about anything you could possibly think of (and many you wouldn't even imagine), from health campaigns and celebrating key people in history to food-related themes.

You can select relevant awareness days to post social media content – anything from an Instagram post or a few Tweets to perhaps hosting a LinkedIn Live event.

Some useful websites for researching awareness days are Days of the Year (www.daysoftheyear.com), On This Day (www.

---

onthisday.com) and This Day in Music (www.thisdayinmusic.com).

It is essential to ensure that you can engage authentically when participating in awareness day-type content. For example, you must be mindful of the concept of rainbow washing, which refers to the practice of using LGBTQ+ symbols like the rainbow flag during events like Pride Month without actively supporting or advocating for the rights and well-being of the LGBTQ+ community throughout the year. When organisations participate in events such as Pride Month, Black History Month or International Women's Day without demonstrating authenticity, there is a potential for backlash from individuals both within and outside the communities being celebrated.

Content curation

'Content curation not only alleviates the pressure of having to devote valuable time to create original content, but it also adds credibility and third-party validations to your efforts.'

Jason Miller, former Group Marketing Manager, Global Content Marketing and Social Media Marketing – LinkedIn

As we saw earlier with the rule of thirds, it's good to share content from other sources. Not only does this save on content creation time, but it shows that you care about learning as much as you can about your subject area and sharing what you find. That's the way to help you be seen as the subject-matter expert or thought leader.

Remember, the content you share on social media should always align with your content pillars.

You can, of course, share content straight from your social media newsfeeds through a repost or Page share. When sharing content, try to add your own comment to give the post some context – it doesn't need to be a long explanation, just enough to let your followers/ connections know your intention and reason for sharing.

When you share content that isn't yours on social media, such as a blog or research statistics, it's essential to approach it ethically and legally. It's important to understand that original content, including images, writing and recordings, is protected by copyright law. Unless you have explicit permission or the content falls under fair use, using it without authorisation is not acceptable. Always provide proper credit and include links to the original source. If you want to use someone else's content, the best practice is to obtain written permission from the creator.

If you're looking for other ways to find content to share, my go-to's are Google Alerts, an RSS reader and Twitter lists. Google Alerts are updates of the latest relevant Google search results – from news and blogs to video and discussion groups – that match your chosen search terms. Alerts can be delivered by email or to an RSS reader as they happen, once a day or once a week if you prefer. They are great for monitoring individuals, organisations, events and other keywords specific to your industry or interests.

To create a Google alert:

1. Go to Google Alerts (www.google.com/alerts).
2. In the box at the top, enter a topic you want to follow.
3. To change your settings, click 'Show Options'. You can change: How often you get notifications. The types of sites you'll see. Your language etc.
4. Click Create Alert.

Many news-related sites, blogs and other online publishers syndicate their content as an RSS feed (RSS stands for Rich Site Summary or Really Simple Syndication). To keep up to date with this content, you'll need an RSS reader. An RSS reader is a software application or online service that allows users to aggregate and organise content from multiple websites or sources into a single location. It saves you from visiting each site separately and provides a streamlined way to stay updated with the latest news. I use Feedly (feedly.com). It's worth spending time seeking out relevant content to add to your reader; I find industry press a great place to start. This also helps to reduce inbox clutter, as you don't need to sign up for each site's email newsletter. I organise my content into subject categories and check it once or twice a day over a cup of coffee. From Feedly, I can schedule and share content directly to my social media profiles.

A Twitter list is a curated collection of Twitter accounts organised based on a theme or topic. Users can create and subscribe to lists to keep track of updates and Tweets from accounts they find interesting or relevant. Lists can be public or private, allowing users to either share their curated collections with others or keep them for personal use. Consider creating a Twitter list for each of your content pillars, which will give you a steady stream of content to Retweet, or act as a source of information for other social media platforms you are using. For a 'how to use Twitter Lists' guide, visit https://help.twitter.com/en/using-twitter/twitter-lists.

User-generated content (UGC)

User-generated content (UGC) refers to any form of content, such as images, videos or reviews, that is created and shared voluntarily by individuals who are not employed or affiliated with a brand or organisation. It is an authentic, organic type of content that is created by users who have had direct experiences with a brand, product or service.

Identifying user-generated content involves actively monitoring social media platforms for mentions and brand-related hashtags (some organisations will create a hashtag specifically to encourage and monitor user-generated content).

It is best practice to request permission to use UGC in your social media marketing activity and to ensure that you give clear credit to the original creator (for example, by tagging them in your post).

User-generated content is incredibly influential in the final stages of the buying decision process when you're looking to convert your audience towards making a purchase. Sharing user-generated content also strengthens the relationship between the brand and its customers. When users see their content being shared or featured by a brand, it creates a sense of appreciation. This fosters a positive brand image, encourages brand loyalty, and motivates users to continue generating content, becoming brand advocates in the process.

Furthermore, using user-generated content provides brands with a diverse range of content that they don't have to create themselves. This content often reflects the genuine experiences, creativity and unique perspectives of users, which can be highly valuable in helping a brand connect with its target audience.

Chapter summary

Effective content is at the heart of social media marketing. When you have meaningful objectives and understand your target audience, you can communicate via a range of different formats, from text to video. Using content pillars ensures a consistent messaging that not only helps you manage your own resources but also ensures that your audience understands your 'why'. The good news is that you do not need to create all the content you share on social media; you can curate from other sources and share content generated by your customers (UGC). You can even share content more than once!

Actions

- Decide on your content pillars and add them to your one-page social media marketing plan template.
- Create a 12-month content calendar. Do some research using a website such as www.daysoftheyear.com, www.onthisday.com and www.thisdayinmusic.com and add key dates relevant to your organisation.
- Create a content inventory spreadsheet. Ensure you keep the inventory up to date: you could add a recurring appointment to your calendar as a reminder to you to check it.
- Build monthly and weekly calendars, as required. You could use an Excel spreadsheet, online planning tools such as Asana (www.asana.com), Trello (www.trello.com) or Monday.com (www.monday.com), or the calendar feature in a social media management tool such as Hootsuite or Sprout Social.
- Look at each social media platform you have chosen to use, and ensure that you know how to find trending content there.
- Decide how you will curate content to share on social media. Set up Google Alerts, subscribe to an RSS feed, create some Twitter lists or whichever methods work for you.
- Make sure you have notifications switched on for mentions of your social media accounts so that you can look out for user-generated content.

Chapter 6

Maximising your social media marketing efforts

In this chapter, we will:

- Learn how to optimise your social media profiles to get found when users are searching online.
- Understand different ways to increase engagement with your social media content.
- Explore the role played by employee advocacy, partnerships and influencers to enhance trust and engagement.

Since over 4 billion people use social media worldwide (DataReportal, January 2023) across various platforms, our ability to reach and engage with individuals and organisations across the world is unrivalled.

But simply having a social media presence and posting content is not enough to guarantee success. 'If you build it, they will come' is a famous line from the Kevin Costner movie *Field of Dreams*, but unfortunately this is not always true in the world of work, especially when it comes to social media.

Many business leaders believe that if they create a social media account, customers will start pouring in, but the reality is often far from it. Social media requires time and effort and needs to be part of a broader marketing strategy. I repeat, social media doesn't work in isolation.

We need to pay attention to detail, put effort into optimising our profiles and content to help them get found and create scroll-stopping content that generates the desired response from our target audience.

Getting found on social media

An emerging trend is the use of social media as a search tool; it is being used as an alternative to search engines. This is particularly common among younger age groups, which means it's likely to increase in importance to social media marketers over the next few years as these groups join the workforce.

We have known, for many years, that customers are carrying out research by themselves – whether by search engine, social media, or asking friends, family and colleagues for recommendations – before making direct contact with an organisation. Content is needed for every stage of the buying process, and it needs to be visible when your target audience is searching for it.

This means that social media is becoming increasingly essential for organisations that are looking to attract and retain customers: it's the marketing channel used by almost 60% of the global population, where they spend several hours each day, and is the preferred media for researching new brands and products and keeping up to date with news and events.

It's easy to follow and connect with users we come across in real life or as we scroll through a newsfeed (especially since each platform makes so many suggestions for users to follow). Nevertheless, it is essential that we proactively pursue opportunities to make ourselves discoverable and to actively grow our follower base on our chosen social media platforms. This starts with how we set up our accounts.

Optimising your profiles

In the offline world, we spend time making a good first impression: for example, in the way we dress for a job interview or a first date. However, online we're often a little, well, lazier. We create an account, fill in a few boxes with our details then log off until we need something, such as a new job. Not spending the time to complete and update your social media profiles is a huge mistake, but it's one made by so many organisations and individuals.

Here are some core guidelines to follow for every social media platform you are using:

- Choose a recognisable username for your account.
- Take a good profile photo (for personal profiles), or use a suitable brand logo (for corporate accounts).
- Add a background/header image to brand your profile.
- Add an 'About' description or bio that clearly explains who you are and how you help your ideal customers.
- Include a link to relevant website page/s.
- Pin/feature relevant posts at the top of your profile.
- Include social proof, such as recommendations, and digital badges e.g. membership of professional bodies or an award-winning sticker.

A social media profile is like a job interview that takes place in under ten seconds. Former president and CEO of Amazon, Jeff Bezos, said: *'Your brand is what people say about you when you're not in the room.'* Your online profile is your brand representative, so it's vital to pay it some attention – and keep it up to date. Social media platforms do have a tendency to add and remove features from accounts, so it's useful to review them at least quarterly.

When you're active on social media – making connections, following accounts, posting content, liking content, etc. – you are inviting people to find out more about you.

And what's the first thing they will do? That's correct. They will check out your profile. So you need to make sure that you're ready to do business. Optimising your social media accounts is not only crucial to help you get found, but it's essential to help you make a good first impression.

The importance of hashtags

The hashtag (#) is one of the most powerful social media features. First used in a Tweet in 2007, hashtags help to group conversations around keywords, phrases and topics. In 2009 Twitter formally adopted the use of hashtags into code, automatically turning words with a # in front of them into clickable links (note, hashtags cannot have spaces). By including hashtags in your social media posts, your content will show up to users who are following or searching those hashtags.

Each social media platform has a different approach to hashtags, and there is varying guidance on best practices and how many to use per post. When using hashtags, relevant words make all the difference, so consider what your target audience might be using when they search.

You can also look at the hashtags your competitors are using. You can identify these by scrolling through their content, or by using a tool such as Semrush Social Tracker. You can also use hashtag research tools such as hashtags.org, hashtagify.me, best-hashtags.com or the app Tagomatic.

As part of your social media marketing planning, I recommend that you research hashtags relevant to your content pillars. You can then pick hashtags from this list as you prepare and post your content.

For example, here's a list of hashtags that you could use for content related to climate change:

- #ClimateChange
- #GlobalWarming
- #ClimateAction
- #Sustainability
- #ZeroWaste
- #ClimateEducation
- #Environment
- #ExtremeWeather
- #SaveThePlanet
- #FaceTheClimateEmergency
- #ClimateChangeIsReal
- #TacklingClimateChange
- #TogetherForOurPlanet
- #OneStepGreener
- #ClimateResearch
- #ClimateCrisis

Luan Wise

Storytelling in three seconds

Traditional storytelling follows a deliberate pace, gradually building up a narrative by introducing characters, settings and conflicts in a methodical manner. It takes time to establish a solid foundation and develop a connection between the audience and the story.

For example, in a timeless fairytale, there once was a brave young girl named Red Riding Hood. She lived in a quaint village nestled deep within a dense forest, surrounded by towering trees and babbling brooks. One day, her grandmother fell ill, and Red Riding Hood set out on a journey through the enchanting woods to deliver a basket of goodies. Little did she know, a cunning wolf lurked behind the trees, plotting to deceive her and satisfy its hunger. As Red Riding Hood ventured deeper into the forest, the conflict between her innocence and the wolf's deceit began to unfold, captivating the audience with each step of her adventure.

Here the deliberate pace of the storytelling allows the audience to immerse themselves in the characters, settings, and conflicts, experiencing the tale's richness and suspense. However, the dynamics of social media are quite different. With its fast-paced nature and the abundance of content competing for people's limited attention spans, it's vital that you capture your audience's interest within the first few seconds. Instead of slowly building up, you need to grab their attention immediately and share your key information early on to keep them reading/watching.

A condensed adaptation of the story would be more suitable on social media. For example, a short video could start with a dramatic shot of Red Riding Hood entering the forest, followed by quick cuts showcasing her encounter with the cunning wolf, before she escapes its clutches and leaves the wolf defeated.

For organisations, storytelling opens up a powerful opportunity to connect with target audiences in a captivating and meaningful way.

Let's consider a corporate software company launching a new productivity tool. Instead of simply showcasing its features, it could leverage storytelling on social media to create an immersive experience for its audience. Through a series of short videos, they could narrate a relatable story of a professional struggling with time management. By introducing their productivity tool as the solution to this common pain point, they create a connection with their target audience, demonstrating the value and benefits of their product in a compelling way.

Additional resources

In his book *Building a Story Brand,* Donald Miller provides a framework for crafting a compelling brand narrative. He emphasises the importance of understanding your customer's desires and positioning them as the hero of the story, and your brand as the guide that helps them overcome obstacles and achieve their goals.

By mastering the art of storytelling on social media, organisations can effectively capture and maintain the attention of their audience, foster brand loyalty, and drive desired actions. The key is to craft narratives that are concise, relatable, and aligned with the target audience's interests, needs, and values.

Dove's Real Beauty campaign is a powerful example of how a brand can position its customers as the hero of their own story. By challenging conventional beauty standards and celebrating diverse representations of beauty, Dove empowers individuals to embrace their unique qualities and feel confident in their own skin. Through inclusive advertising campaigns and initiatives, Dove showcases real people from all walks of life, encouraging self-acceptance and promoting a positive body image.

Visit www.dove.com/uk/stories/campaigns.html to learn more about Dove's campaigns and how they are helping to make beauty a source of confidence, not anxiety.

Algorithms

A social media algorithm refers to the complex set of rules and calculations used by social media platforms to determine the content that users see on their feeds. Algorithms are designed to curate and personalise the content shown to users based on their interests, preferences, past behaviour and engagement patterns. How algorithms work depends on the social media platform: the exact details are unknown and change constantly.

You might have noticed that the word 'algorithm' has hardly been used throughout this book. This is deliberate: I read and hear far too many conversations about 'hacking the algorithms'; I am not a fan of taking this approach or using algorithm changes as an excuse for poor performance. Information about 'hacks' tends to overwhelm rather than advance the use of social media.

My preferred approach is to focus on your business, your objectives, and what your target audience needs. I advise you to keep up with news and trends and look for the answers to your questions within your own data. Additionally, implementing a testing approach can provide valuable insights to help optimise your social media activity. More on testing in Chapter 7.

Stopping the scroll

To capture the attention of users scrolling through their feeds and prompt them to pause and pay attention to your content, you need to create a 'thumb-stopping moment'. This could be through the use of a bold headline, an interesting visual or a moving image (e.g. video).

Back in our Chapter 2 case study, we saw how testing different creative options led Cheltenham Borough Council to always post content with a video, image or photo to accompany it. They found that this approach was much more popular than content posted without an image, photo or video. For this council, posting text only received little or no engagement. Testing what works for you and your organisation is key.

Here are some suggestions to help create a 'thumb-stopping moment' with your social media content:

- **Maintain a consistent look and feel across your social media posts**

  Establishing a consistent look and feel across your social media platforms is central to creating a strong brand identity and connecting with your audience. If you have brand guidelines for your organisation – for example, colours, fonts and visual elements – you should use these across all social media. You may find that you need to expand your guidelines to create relevant templates for social media content if they are not already included. 'Tone of voice' is also important, this refers to the personality, style and language you use in your marketing messages. When your social media posts become instantly recognisable, your audience will pay attention.

- **Use high-quality images**

  Ideally, take your own photos so that you can show your products and people authentically. If you need to use stock library resources, take your time to look for images that align with your brand, and avoid anything that looks overly staged or clichéd (and check you have the correct usage rights). Each social media platform has its own preferred sizing for images and video, which can be frustrating. But, it's important to make sure that you prepare artwork correctly. There's nothing worse than a cut-off headline or an image that's missing a part.

  You can find always up-to-date information on image and video requirements at www.sproutsocial.com/insights/social-media-image-sizes-guide/ and www.sproutsocial.com/insights/social-media-video-specs-guide/.

- **Embrace diversity and inclusion**

  In all content, it is essential to ensure inclusivity by representing a diverse range of individuals and communities. When you intentionally include people with different backgrounds, ethnicities, sexes, ages, abilities and body types, you create a sense of belonging and foster a connection with a wider audience.

Case study: Monzo

Monzo is an online bank based in the UK. In 2017 it secured £1 million of investment in a record-breaking 96 seconds via crowdfunding. Now more than 7 million people in the UK use

Monzo to spend and manage their money, with hundreds more joining every day.

Monzo has a strong presence on social media platforms like Twitter, Instagram and Facebook, where it engages with customers and shares updates about its products and services. You can follow them: @Monzo

On social media, Monzo has developed a unique, engaging tone of voice that appeals to younger customers. The company uses humour and relatable content to connect with its audience and create a sense of community among its customers. For example, Monzo often shares memes and jokes on its social media accounts, which has helped it to create a human, approachable brand image.

You can read Monzo's tone of voice guidelines at https://monzo.com/tone-of-voice/.

Tailoring social media content to different platforms

Tailoring social media content to the nuance of each platform is necessary to maximise engagement and connect with each platform's audience. Each social media platform has its own style, requiring a thoughtful approach to adapt your content effectively.

For instance, LinkedIn, as a professional networking platform, requires a more formal, business-oriented tone. Tailor your content to LinkedIn by sharing industry-specific knowledge, professional insights and thought leadership. Engage with professionals through meaningful discussions, participate in relevant groups, and showcase your expertise through long-form articles or LinkedIn Live events.

Twitter, on the other hand, is known for its fast-paced, concise nature. To tailor content for Twitter, keep your messages short and impactful, and utilise hashtags and mentions to increase your discoverability. Engage with your audience through real-time conversations, Retweets, and sharing valuable industry insights or breaking news.

Facebook is suitable for various types of content. You can share a mix of images and videos, plus links to blog posts and other website pages. Engage with your audience through comments, likes and shares. You can also participate in relevant group conversations.

Instagram is a visually driven platform where high-quality images and aesthetically pleasing content perform well. Consider utilising features like carousel posts on the feed, Story stickers or Instagram Live to provide interactive content experiences.

Your content on TikTok should reflect the platform's light-hearted, trend-driven nature, with a focus on quick storytelling, humour and captivating visuals. Use engaging soundtracks and visually appealing effects to connect with the TikTok community and trends.

With Snapchat's emphasis on real-time updates and personal interactions, your content should feel like a genuine conversation with your audience. Share behind-the-scenes glimpses, exclusive offers or sneak peeks to make your followers feel as if they're part of an exclusive community. Use a friendly, conversational tone, incorporating emojis, filters and augmented reality features to enhance the interactive experience.

Sometimes your social media content plan will include posting the same messages across different platforms: this is fine so long as it aligns with the preferences of your target audience and the characteristics of the platform. You will, however, need to adapt your post for each platform. It's all too obvious if a post has been posted on multiple platforms without adapting it. For example, you would say 'link in bio' on Instagram, but on Facebook, you would include a link in the post. It's also preferable to remove watermarks when you create a TikTok and want to post the same video on another platform.

A note about multiple accounts

I'm often asked whether it's acceptable to have multiple accounts on a single social media platform. The answer is, 'it depends on the platform'. For example, individuals should only have one LinkedIn profile (as per the platforms' terms and conditions).

As well as needing the time and resources to manage multiple accounts, it is important to establish whether you have an audience and the need for multiple accounts before setting them up. If you're not sure what to do, take a look at what your competitors are doing. Do they have multiple accounts? Also, review the type of responses and messages you are receiving from your audiences – what do they need from you? If you think it might be too complex to manage multiple accounts, consider how you might unify your content. Whatever you decide, please ensure that you focus on your audience, and not on how your organisation (and its silos) are structured.

Some organisations do opt for multiple accounts, particularly on Twitter and Instagram. People like to follow accounts that post topics that interest them, so if you have truly distinct messages to send, creating separate accounts can be a great way to be more relevant to the needs of your target audiences.

On these social media platforms, you could consider having:
- a corporate account – dedicated to providing updates on your organisation as a whole
a customer service account – where you can resolve complaints and answer questions and comments
- a product-led account – to provide product news and information: for example, retailers could have separate accounts for clothing and homeware
- audience-led accounts – focused on the needs of a target audience: for example, this could be location-specific if your organisation is international, or subject-specific for higher education establishments.

I once facilitated a workshop at an event venue to discuss its social media presence. The venue hosted a variety of events, from weddings to corporate conferences. Creating a Twitter account for each type of event would be too time-consuming to manage, but sharing wedding information alongside information on corporate events could alienate an audience. The workshop concluded by deciding to focus content-sharing on the venue, to emphasise its versatility. It's a well-known venue in the local area, so by highlighting 'what's on' and key features such as food, staff and service, which make the venue the right choice for any occasion, the Twitter account could stay manageable and meet the interests of a wider audience.

Accessibility – best practice

Approximately 15% of people worldwide experience some form of disability, so it's important not to unintentionally exclude anyone from understanding your social media posts.

By making your content more accessible, you ensure a better experience for everyone.

To make your social media posts more accessible, consider implementing these simple changes:

- **Keep your posts simple:** Stick to short sentences, limit the use of excessive text, and incorporate line breaks to create a visually appealing, easy-to-read format.
- **Avoid formatting distractions:** Minimise the use of bold, italics, capitals and special symbols that can make the content difficult to read or understand.
- **Use emojis thoughtfully:** Emojis can add visual interest to your posts, but avoid relying on them to convey essential information. Their meaning can be easily misinterpreted, so use them sparingly and ensure they complement the text rather than replace it. If you're not sure what emojis are suitable, visit www.emojipedia.com.
- **Think about typeface and colours:** Ensure that your text and background colours have a sufficient contrast to make the content readable for people with visual impairments. Use a colour contrast analyser (such as https://color.adobe.com/create/color-contrast-analyzer from Adobe) to check if your images meet accessibility standards.
- **Alt text:** Provide alternative text (alt text) for images to describe their content and context. Focus on conveying the meaning of the image rather than providing excessive details. Alt text is essential for individuals who are blind or partially sighted to understand the visual elements in your posts when using a screen reader. A useful tool to help create alt text is https://alttext.ai.
- **Consider captions/subtitles:** You should include captions/subtitles in videos to make them accessible to individuals who are deaf or have some hearing loss. Additionally, consider

adding a voiceover to describe on-screen actions or visuals. Make sure that captions are concise, easily readable, and provide a clear understanding of the video's content.

- **Use camel case for hashtags:** Capitalise the first letter of each word in hashtags to enhance readability for assistive technology. For example, use #BlackLivesMatter instead of #blacklivesmatter. This helps to distinguish individual words within hashtags.

Growing your social media following

Growing your social media following is essential for increasing awareness and credibility. While it's good to know that your online audience is increasing in number, maintaining authenticity, engagement, and quality interactions with your audience should remain the primary focus.

Various online services promise to provide thousands of followers – for a fee. However, buying followers is not considered best practice, so please don't take this approach. I have included the information here solely to help you in any conversations you might have on this topic.

First, most of the followers obtained through these services are fake or bot accounts, which means they don't represent genuine engagement or interest in your content. This is because these accounts are created solely for the purpose of boosting follower counts. They are unlikely to interact with your posts, purchase your products or services, or become loyal fans.

Second, social media algorithms are designed to prioritise content that receives high levels of engagement, such as likes, comments and shares. When a large portion of your followers are fake or inactive, your engagement rates will suffer, and your content may be deprioritised by the algorithm, making it harder for genuine followers to see your posts.

Third, social media platforms have strict policies against buying fake followers and engagement. If you are caught buying followers, your account may be penalised or even banned, which could harm your reputation and impact your ability to reach genuine followers and customers in the future.

Instead of buying followers, it is better to focus on building a genuine following through organic growth strategies such as creating quality content, engaging with your audience and collaborating with other accounts in your niche. This approach may take longer to produce results, but it will result in a more engaged, loyal following – and this is more likely to benefit your organisation in the long run.

Increasing social media engagement

To increase engagement with your social media content, it's essential to go beyond simply capturing your audience's attention. Engagement involves gaining their interest, sparking conversations, and encouraging them to take action. If you recall from Chapter 1, this is how TikTok saw early growth of the platform; by setting challenges for its users to get involved with. Posting content without considering how to get your audience involved is unlikely to achieve the results you want.

Engagement on social media is measured by actions such as video views, likes, comments and shares. These actions can have a domino effect, as they not only amplify your content but also generate further engagement through increased visibility and participation. The key is to create content that prompts your audience to think, feel, and do something.

Including all the necessary details in your social media posts is vital to facilitate engagement. If you're promoting a webinar, for example, ensure that you provide information such as dates, times, locations, booking instructions or links to additional resources. By addressing the 'who', 'what', 'where', 'why', 'when' and 'how' in your content, you minimise the chance that you will omit important details – and you maximise the audience's ability to engage with your post easily.

Are competitions a good idea for social media content?

Yes! Hosting competitions on social media can be a good tactic to promote your products and engage your social media audience.

Competitions can take various forms, such as photo contests, caption contests, quizzes or creative challenges. Offering your own products or other enticing prizes, you can create a buzz and generate interest among your audience. The prize does not need to be of high value.

The method of entering competitions is usually based on liking/ following your social media account, so this is a great help in building your following.

When you are running a competition via social media, you must consider the promotional policies of the platform/s you are using – these will guide how you run the promotion, including how people can enter. You must include terms and conditions and comply with the promotional marketing codes of practice for your country.

Here are some useful links to ensure your competition complies with best practices:

- Facebook terms and policies: https://www.facebook.com/policies_center/pages_groups_events/
- Instagram promotion guidelines: https://help.instagram.com/179379842258600
- Twitter guidelines for promotions: https://help.twitter.com/en/rules-and-policies/twitter-contest-rules
- UK competition guidelines: https://www.asa.org.uk/advice-online/promotional-marketing-prize-draws-in-social-media.html

The art of conversation

Conversations on social media play a key role in building an engaged audience and fostering meaningful connections.

When it comes to starting a conversation, it's important to write content that encourages participation. One effective way to initiate a dialogue is by asking a thought-provoking question. For instance, if you're a travel company, you could post an image of some breathtaking scenery and ask your audience, 'What's your dream holiday location?' This prompts followers to share their opinions and experiences and engages them in a conversation.

To get involved in an existing conversation, actively comment on other people's content. Instead of simply liking a post, take the time to leave a thoughtful comment that adds value to the discussion. For example, if you come across a post about a new book release, you could comment 'This book sounds fascinating! Has anyone read it yet?

I'd love to hear your thoughts.' (Yes, this is a hint – I would appreciate comments about this book on social media!)

By expressing genuine interest and seeking others' opinions, you encourage engagement and create opportunities for meaningful interactions.

Michelle Goodall, Chief Marketing Officer for the professional networking and community app Guild (www.guild.co), uses the word 'community' to suggest connectedness, togetherness, people joining in and becoming something bigger than the sum of their parts.

Engaging in conversations on social media helps to build your audience in several ways. It allows you to establish yourself as an active, valuable participant in your community. By consistently offering insightful comments and initiating engaging discussions, you position yourself as the subject-matter expert or thought leader.

Actively participating in conversations on profiles, pages and within groups/communities also increases your visibility to a wider audience. When you comment, your username and profile picture become visible to their followers, potentially leading them to check out your profile and follow you.

It's useful to understand that not all discussions need to be conducted in the public domain. Initiating and engaging in private conversations through direct messages can provide a more personalised setting for deeper interactions. By reaching out to your connections individually, you can establish a stronger rapport and have more meaningful exchanges. Transitioning from text-based conversations to real-time interactions, whether it's a face-to-face meeting or a virtual call, adds a new level of depth and authenticity to a relationship.

Getting the timing right

When is the best time to post on social media? This is a common question, and - yes -the most accurate answer lies within your own data.

It's valuable to consider when your audience is most active online, as social media moves at a rapid pace, and timing plays a significant role in maximising opportunities for engagement. It's likely that your 'best time' will differ for each social media platform.

Facebook, Instagram and TikTok offer insights and data on viewer behaviour. On Facebook, navigate to 'Insights' and select 'Posts' to access information about when your audience is online. Instagram's business accounts provide similar data in the insights section, accessible via the graph icon in the top right corner of the app. Figure 6.1 shows a screenshot of the 'most active times' information on Instagram. You can select to see information for each day of the week; sometimes you might spot one or two days that have more activity than others. You can also look at the most active times for each day. Here we can see that on Mondays, followers of this account are most active at 6 p.m. Most are unlikely to be online between midnight and 6 a.m. It would be sensible for the owners of this account to post their content later in the day.

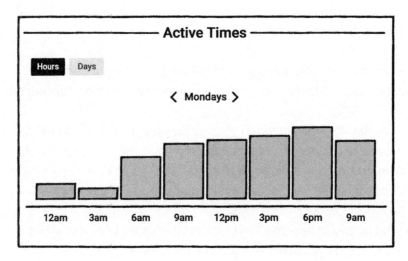

Figure 6.1. Most active times (Instagram Insights).

If you lack sufficient data of your own, you can turn to industry research for guidance. Better still, carry out your own tests to identify the days and times that will drive the highest reach and engagement for your social media accounts. You should balance these insights with your own working patterns, as you need to ensure that you are available to respond promptly to any comments.

Most social media platforms now have the option to schedule content natively (i.e. directly on the platform). However, when you are managing multiple accounts across different platforms, tools such as Hootsuite or Sprout Social provide valuable assistance in optimising your social media presence. These tools allow you to plan, schedule and automate your content postings, ensuring that they are shared at the most relevant times for your organisation.

Calls to action

Don't forget to tell people what they should do in response to your social media post. Should they contact you to arrange a meeting?

Should they visit your website to download a useful resource (where you can capture their contact details)?

If you want your audience to do something in response to seeing a social media post, it's a good idea to be clear and let them know what you want them to do next. We call this a call to action, or CTA.

A call to action should use active words. Here's a list of examples that you might include:

- Call now
- Find out more
- Visit a store today
- Visit our website
- Click here
- Learn more
- Read more
- Watch this video
- Try out this demo
- Listen to this podcast
- Register
- Sign up
- Enrol
- Join
- Subscribe
- Download
- Get started
- Share
- Buy
- Shop
- Donate

Is your website ready to convert visitors?

Social media is an excellent way to drive traffic to your website. By including links to your website in your social media posts, you can direct your audience to visit a product page, read a blog, download a document, register for an event, etc.

For best results, your website must be ready for the visitors that arrive from social media. This is often a problem, and I've stalled many social media marketing plans on the basis that a website needs to be updated before posting links that will drive additional visitors to it.

If your website is not ready for conversion, you will be wasting time and effort by driving potential customers there. If you are paying for advertisements, you could also be wasting a lot of money.

Does it include social proof - evidence that other people have purchased and found value in your products and services - in terms of recommendations and reviews?

You also need to ensure that your website works well, technically. For example, do the pages load quickly? Is the mobile experience good?

Here are two useful (free) tools for you to check your website:

Ahrefs broken link checker: https://ahrefs.com/broken-link-checker

GTmetrix website performance testing and monitoring tool: https://gtmetrix.com

Leveraging social media mentions

Involving others with your social media content through mentions is a powerful way to engage and connect with individuals, organisations or communities. Mentioning someone in your social media posts involves tagging their username, and directly referencing them in your content.

When you mention an organisation or individual, you bring their attention to your post, acknowledging their contribution, involvement or relevance to the topic being discussed. This allows you to show appreciation, give credit or highlight collaborations, thereby strengthening relationships with individuals or organisations within your network.

This can also attract attention from the mentioned user's followers, increasing the potential for engagement, likes, comments and shares on your content. It also encourages reciprocation, as the mentioned user will hopefully respond to or share your post, further amplifying its reach.

Employee advocacy

Employee advocacy means the promotion of a company's brand, products or services by its employees through social media and other online channels. In other words, it is the practice of encouraging and empowering employees to share company-related content on their personal social media profiles, to increase the reach and credibility of the company's message.

The LinkedIn Official Guide to Employee Advocacy shares some statistics that support the value of this approach:

- On average, employees have 10 times more 1st-degree connections on LinkedIn than a company Page has followers.
- We're 8 times more likely to engage with content shared by employees than content shared by brands.
- We're 24 times more likely to reshare content shared by employees than content shared by brands.
- Content is clicked through twice as often when it's shared by employees.

An employee advocacy programme should include training and ongoing support to help employees maintain their visibility while supporting the organisation's online presence. Training is also valuable in allaying and overcoming fears that are involved with using social media at work. Consider how you can provide colleagues and partners with preapproved content, such as blog posts, infographics or videos, that they can share on social media. It's also useful to recognise and reward employees who actively participate and share content – there's nothing like tapping into their competitiveness to get people involved!

We discussed this topic during the qualitative research interviews in both 2020 and 2022. Here's a few soundbites that might resonate, and provide some reassurance:

> **If people use social media in everyday life,
> they are much more receptive and willing to use social media in the workplace.**

> **My first few years in the role were spent convincing people we need to be using it [social media].
> Thankfully, now everyone sees value in social media and my job is so much easier.**

> **Since the [LinkedIn] training, there has been more engagement from employees. They have a bit more understanding and see the value of LinkedIn.
> We've also seen an upsurge in followers on our company Page since everyone has been more active on their personal profiles.**

The power of partnerships and influencers

In the world of social media, partnerships and influencers play a pivotal role in supporting the reach and impact of content.

Partnerships can take various forms, such as cross-promotions, joint content creation or co-hosted events.

Cross-promotions are where two or more brands or individuals join forces to promote each other's content or products. This can include sharing each other's posts, featuring one another in videos or blog articles or engaging in joint advertising campaigns. By leveraging each partner's existing audience, cross-promotions can effectively expand the reach and visibility of both parties, exposing them to new potential followers or customers.

Some social media platforms have introduced collaboration features to encourage and facilitate joint content creation. For example, Instagram announced Collab posts in late 2021, allowing two accounts to share a feed post or Reel.

When we discussed the decision-making unit in Chapter 3, we included influencers. The term influencer is also used to describe individuals who have built a significant online following and have an influence over their audience's opinions and behaviours. There are different types of influencers, ranging from nano-influencers (who have a small but highly engaged following) to micro-influencers (who have a more moderate reach) and macro-influencers (who boast a larger audience and broader influence).

Influencers promote products and lifestyles through content on social media. They work to build relationships with their followers; in turn, they can use their audience to generate income.

Working with influencers can take various forms, such as sponsored content, brand collaborations or ambassador programmes. Through these partnerships, influencers can share your brand's message, products or services with their followers, generating buzz and sparking conversations. Leveraging the power of influencers, and the trust they have with their followers, allows brands to connect with new audiences, drive engagement, and maximise the impact of their social media content.

Case study: Mrs Hinch

Mrs Hinch (real name Sophie Hinchliffe) is a popular social media influencer known for her cleaning tips and home organisation content. With her friendly and relatable approach, she has amassed a large following across various social media platforms, particularly Instagram.

Mrs Hinch started sharing her cleaning routines, favourite products and organising hacks in 2018. Just three months after creating her account, Mrs Hinch had one million followers. Her content resonated with users seeking cleaning inspiration and tips. As her following grew, Mrs Hinch established a strong community of like-minded individuals who referred to themselves as 'Hinchers', sharing their own cleaning achievements and seeking advice from Mrs Hinch and fellow community members.

As a result of her growing audience and popularity, Mrs Hinch has collaborated with various brands, written books, and even launched her own range of cleaning and homeware products.

Her recommendations and endorsements have had a significant impact on consumer behaviour, raising brand awareness and driving product sales.

Follow @mrshinchhome on Instagram.

Additional resources

Influencer Marketing Hub offers a wealth of resources, including guides, case studies and tools, to help you navigate the world of influencer marketing. Visit its website at: https://influencermarketinghub.com/.

Chapter summary

This chapter has been packed with ways for you to maximise the impact of your social media marketing efforts, from optimising your social media profiles to paying attention to detail when preparing your content.

We have explored different ways to increase engagement with content, including accessibility best practices and the art of conversation. We have also learned how to collaborate with others, from colleagues to external partners and influencers.

Actions

- Diarise a recurring appointment to review your account set-ups (perhaps quarterly).

- If you do not have brand or tone of voice guidelines, review the example from Monzo. You will find other examples if you search online. Check that any existing guidelines include information about social media content.
- Do some hashtag research for each of your content pillars. Use tools such as hashtags.org, hashtagify.me, best-hashtags.com or the app Tagomatic. Add the list of hashtags to your one-page social media marketing plan, and save them in a Notes file or a Word file for easy access when you are posting content.
- Look through your social media accounts to identify where you can implement best practices, including a consistent visual style, correct image sizing, and tailoring for each platform. How inclusive and accessible is your content? Try experiencing your social media posts via a screen reader, watching videos with your eyes closed, and using a colour contrast checker to review your images.
- Add a list of relevant calls to action to your one-page social media marketing plan.
- Look at your social media account insights to discover when your audience is most active. Add to your one-page social media marketing plan the best times to post. If you do not have account insights, search for industry reports and set out a plan to test what works best for you.
- Review your website. Start with checking technical issues, such as broken links and site speed. Then put yourselves in your customer's shoes and see how easy your site is to navigate. Can you find the information you want to find? Referring back to your content inventory will help with this exercise.
- Create a list of individuals and organisations you might mention in your social media posts. Add the usernames to your one-page social media marketing plan.

- Consider how you might involve your colleagues with social media. Could you set up an employee advocacy programme?
- Who might you collaborate with? Are influencers right for your organisation? Schedule some time to research potential partnerships and create an action plan to explore potential opportunities.

Chapter 7

Understanding the measurements that matter

In this chapter, we will:

- Recognise the challenges of social media measurement.
- Understand the key measurements that align with the buying decision process.
- Explore how to share results with key stakeholders.

Marketing activity has never been easy to measure, and the infamous and frequently quoted statement from US department store merchant Jon Wanamaker – 'Half the money I spend on advertising is wasted; the trouble is, I don't know which half' – rings true.

When reviewing social media marketing, we often start with counting – looking at the number of posts, clicks, likes and shares, for example. This is relatively easy (when you know where to look). True measurement dives deeper by analysing both the numbers (quantitative measures) and qualitative aspects of social media, such as context and sentiment.

Social media is simultaneously the most measurable marketing channel and the one that is most difficult to assess. This paradox arises due to the vast amount of data available from social media platforms and via third-party applications. But the availability of data is not the issue. The challenge lies in the complexity of working with multiple platforms (all of which provide data in different formats) and the difficulty of attributing specific actions to specific pieces of social media activity. Plus, there are many touchpoints throughout the buying decision process, not just from social media, meaning that attributing success to any single piece of marketing activity is unrealistic.

Social media is a big investment

As part of our research, we asked marketers about the level of investment that social media represents. The results are shown in Figure 7.1. In 2020 76.3% agreed that it was a big investment, with 8.4% disagreeing or strongly disagreeing. 2022 saw an increase to 89.4% of respondents in agreement, with 6.7% disagreeing or strongly disagreeing.

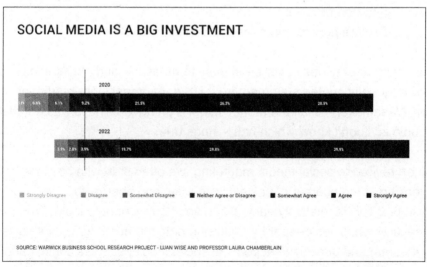

Figure 7.1. Responses to the statement, 'Social media is a big investment.'

When we're investing so heavily in social media, we need to ensure that our actions are working and making an impact; achieving our objectives, – and that they are in alignment with our business plan. We need to measure results and report to key stakeholders.

When we asked respondents to our online questionnaire about knowing what to measure, over half (58.3% in 2020 and 55.1% in 2022) did know what to measure. This is shown in Figure 7.2. However, this also means that just under half didn't know what to measure, which corresponds with the response to the question about knowing how to set the right social media objectives (see Figure 2.4).

This statistic is concerning. However, by the end of this book, you should be able to answer these questions and know how to set the right objectives and what to measure.

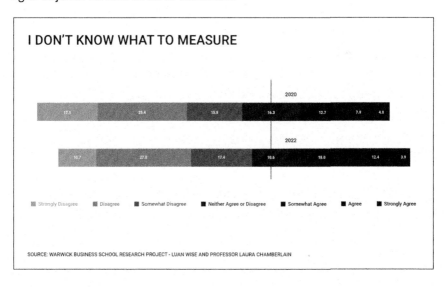

Figure 7.2. Responses to the statement, 'I don't know what to measure.'

Knowing what *can* and *cannot* be measured is also essential. Just like traditional media, a lot of the added value of social media will never be measurable. While traditional media channels like television or print advertising often rely on measurements such as ratings or circulation numbers, they also recognise the intangible benefits that contribute to their overall impact. Similarly, social media platforms offer unique advantages such as building brand awareness and fostering customer loyalty. Intangible aspects, such as brand reputation, emotional connections or word-of-mouth influence are difficult to capture through numbers alone.

As we saw with the Aimia research (Chapter 3), there are large numbers of social media users (onlookers) who are influenced by social media, but who never interact online. Users who don't interact with you directly on social media may still be influenced by your content and may purchase in-store or refer you to a colleague or friend, for example.

There is also a need to distinguish between the short-term and long-term effects of social media activity. For example, activities such as competitions will inevitably result in greater immediate engagement, but they may not provide beneficial long-term effects such as brand loyalty and repeat purchases. Building trust within your network, and cultivating a community, take time.

Measuring the effectiveness of social media

Measuring the effectiveness of social media refers to an assessment of its impact on your goals and objectives.

Understanding what you are getting back from the time, money and resource you're putting into social media activities is critical. The key factor to bear in mind is that you only need to measure what matters to your organisation.

- It matters if it's helping you achieve your business goals.

- It matters if you know what to do next when you look at the measurement.

'Begin with the end in mind' is the second of the seven habits of highly effective people Dr Stephen R. Covey defines in his bestselling book of the same name, and this is a good rule of thumb when it comes to deciding what to measure. In Chapter 2 we looked at the importance of aligning our social media marketing plan with the business plan and setting meaningful objectives.

This is the best approach to social media measurement; all too often I see requests for social media data at the end of a campaign period when they haven't been set out in advance. It's essential to ask questions about what success looks like whenever you are starting a new campaign and to ensure that you have reporting templates and tools in place to help you measure what matters to your organisation. It's not always possible to gather the information you need afterwards. For example, if you wanted to use a branded hashtag and measure its reach, you would need to ensure that it is all set up from the beginning of your campaign, and included in every post.

There are several measurements that can help us understand the effectiveness of our social media activity: follower numbers, audience insights, awareness, engagement, website traffic and lead generation. Let's look at each of these in turn. We'll then look at what to do when we have these measurements.

Follower numbers

Social media measurement is often considered in terms of audience size – the number of Facebook page likes or Twitter followers you might have. This is often the first question asked by a business leader (when they have no detailed knowledge of social media).

You do, of course, need followers. This data does have its place: for example, it's good to know the size of the opportunity and to aim high in terms of audience-building. After all, why stop at 3,000 followers on Twitter if the leading trade magazine in your industry has 40,000?

However, audience size does not give any indication of quality or impact, which is why it is often referred to as a 'vanity metric'.

When asked about how success is measured during our qualitative interviews one respondent focused on followers as the primary metric. They said:

As long as our audience is growing, it's OK.

To measure follower growth, look at the number of new followers you have (we call this net new followers) over a reporting period, then divide by your total audience and multiply by 100 to get your audience growth rate percentage. You should do this for each social media platform you use (Figure 7.3):

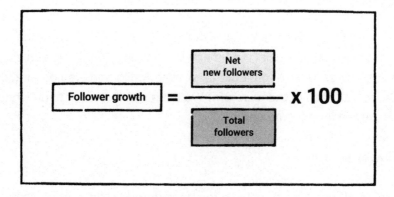

Figure 7.3. How to calculate follower growth.

These calculations would also be valuable when you are examining your social media competition. How does your follower growth compare to your competitors, for example?

Audience insights

Another valuable insight is the profile of your followers. Do they match your target audience criteria? It doesn't matter how many followers you have if they are not the right fit.

For example, checking insights on your Facebook page, Instagram, TikTok and Snapchat accounts will provide you with information about the age, sex and location of your followers. (You will need to switch to a professional account on Instagram, TikTok and Snapchat to access these Insights.) Audience profile data is not currently available for Twitter, and LinkedIn follower data is only available for Pages. LinkedIn company Page data offers insights into location, job function, seniority, industry and company size. For a LinkedIn personal profile you can view details for the job titles of people who found you through search, and for content you post you can view demographics of unique viewers by job title, location, company name, industry and company size.

In Figure 7.4, which is taken from Facebook Insights, we can see that most of the audience on this page is female (87.9%). The majority are aged 35–54, and UK based. This aligns with our target audience profile. If there was a mismatch between the audience data and your expectations, you would then need to review why this might be the case, and consider your next steps. Is your content appealing to the wrong profile, perhaps?

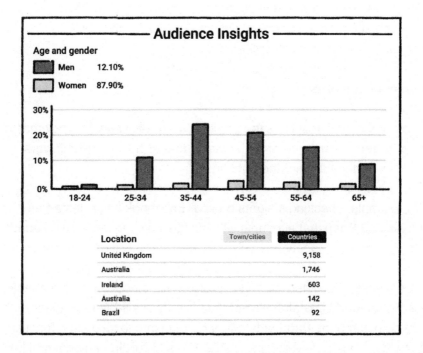

Figure 7.4. Example audience insights for a Facebook page.

Awareness

Awareness refers to the extent to which a message is reaching your target audience: it's about visibility. To measure awareness, we can look at data for reach and impressions. For video content, we would consider video views – that is, the number of times a video is started.

Some platforms provide data on reach, while others provide data on impressions. It's important to check what data you are looking at, and ensure you understand how the data is gathered:

- **Reach** refers to the total number of followers/connections who have the chance to see your posts at any given point in time. In a perfect world, this would be every one of your followers, but that is not the case, due to the way the social media platform algorithms work. Your posts can also be shown to non-followers: this is especially the case with the 'For You' page on TikTok and, more recently, Twitter.

- **Impressions** are the number of times your content is displayed in newsfeeds. For example, a LinkedIn post could show up in the original author's newsfeed, and appear again when someone shares the post. If you saw both posts in your feed – from the original author, and via a connection – that would count as two impressions for the same post. A viewer does not have to engage with a post for it to count as an impression.

As your audience begin to share your posts, your reach and impressions will increase, which naturally leads to increased awareness. When someone shares a post, it means they found it valuable. It also means that they found it so valuable that they're willing to attach their own brand/reputation to it as they pass it along. This is why encouraging your audience to take action and share your content is so important. We call this engagement.

Engagement

Social media engagement measures how much people interact with your content. It's a measure for the 'social' part of social media and can include likes, shares, link clicks, mentions, comments, replies, direct (private) messages and video completions (watching a video to the end).

Since social media algorithms are said to prioritise showing posts in newsfeeds using engagement such as likes, comments and shares as a signal, it's an important quality measure to focus on. However, engagement data is often low and erratic.

In Chapter 6 we noted the importance of engagement to increase your visibility to a wider audience.

The total number of engagements on a social media post is useful, but it is far better to calculate an engagement rate. There are different ways to do this. I prefer to use a formula that takes into account followers and to calculate the percentage of followers who chose to interact with the content after seeing it. An alternative is to calculate the percentage of those reached who chose to interact with the content after seeing it. Either way, by calculating a percentage you will get a figure that is easier to compare, especially over time and in comparison to competitor data.

You can calculate the engagement rate of an individual post or as an average for all posts across a defined reporting period. To do this you will need to know the total number of engagements (likes, comments, shares) and the number of followers you have on a particular platform. This calculation is shown in Figure 7.5.

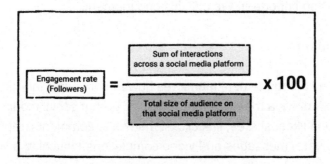

Figure 7.5. How to calculate engagement rate, based on followers.

A lower engagement rate means that your post wasn't interesting enough for audiences to take action after seeing it in their feed, or perhaps a call to action was missing so they didn't know what you wanted them to do next. A higher engagement rate would indicate that your post was of interest to your audience – and you should consider posting more of this type of content. From your calculations you will need to determine what is your average, and then what you consider to be 'low' or 'high'. The best answers are in your own data.

This calculation is useful as part of competitor analysis. How does your engagement compare to others in your industry? Greater engagement is, in my opinion, far more valuable than follower numbers. It's also something that's important to monitor as you grow your audience and try out different types of content or new features.

Additional resources

Download an up-to-date *Guide to Native Social Media Analytics* (including how to set key performance indicators and a reporting template) by visiting by my website at www.luanwise.co.uk/books/planning-for-success/social-media-analytics or scanning the QR code below:

Website traffic

If your goal is to drive traffic to your website, then you need to track link clicks. Link data is provided by social media platforms or third-party scheduling tools such as Hootsuite and Sprout Social. It is available for both organic and paid-for posts.

When a social media user reaches your website, you can gather detailed data by using Google Analytics.

Google Analytics records every visit to your website (unless a user has switched off tracking codes and cookies), and information about where visitors came from, if they are a new or returning visitor, what pages they viewed, how long they spent on your website, and more. The death of third-party cookies poses additional challenges to measuring website traffic. (Third-party cookies are small text files stored by websites other than the one being visited, allowing advertisers to track user behaviour and collect data across multiple websites. However, due to privacy concerns and evolving regulations, major web browsers like Chrome, Safari, and Firefox have taken steps to limit or eliminate the use of third-party cookies.)

In Chapter 6 I asked the question, is your website ready to convert visitors? You will be wasting efforts on driving traffic to your website via social media if your website is not set up for the next step.

Additional resources

Skillshop is a free Google training platform that you can use to learn more about tools such as Google Analytics. Visit: https://skillshop.withgoogle.com/

Lead generation

Lead generation refers to the process of identifying and capturing potential customers or leads who have shown interest in a product, service or brand. It's particularly relevant for B2B marketing, where the sales cycle can take longer than in B2C purchases.

When we talk about lead generation via social media, this could refer to form submissions, email sign-ups or other actions that indicate interest in a product or service. These actions all serve as valuable touchpoints in the marketing funnel, allowing organisations to capture potential leads and nurture them towards making a purchase (for example, using email marketing or retargeting; a marketing tactic that involves displaying advertisements to people who have previously interacted with a social media account or visited a website).

By accessing insights from social media platforms and tools like Google Analytics, you can measure visits to your website and new email subscribers, for example. The calls to action you use as part of your social media content will guide your lead generation measurements. That's why 'start with the end in mind' is such a good guide. Know what you want to measure, then measure it!

How to calculate social media return on investment (ROI)

This chapter is all about proving the value of social media to your organisation's overall goals and objectives, and it wouldn't be complete without a return on investment (ROI) calculation: ROI is a performance measure that looks at the benefit (or return) of doing something.

We asked, 'How do you measure social media return on investment?' as part of our research (Figure 7.6), and discovered that fewer people measured ROI in 2022 than in 2020. This is another worrying finding; I hope that, after reading this book, you would give a different answer.

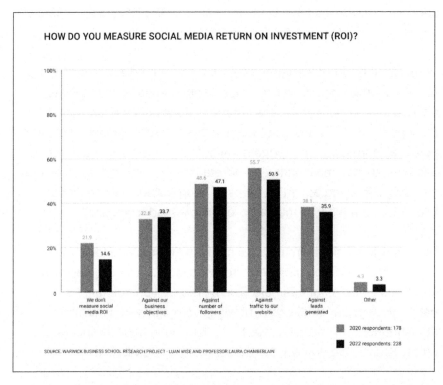

Figure 7.6. How respondents measured social media return on investment.

Respondents were able to select more than one answer to this question. The most popular response was to measure ROI by traffic, followed by number of followers, then leads generated. 'Measurement against objectives' saw the only increase between 2020 and 2022, but was the answer for just a third of respondents.

ROI is usually calculated by subtracting the cost of doing something from the value you're creating (such as a lead or a sale), and dividing the cost of the investment, then multiplying it by 100 to get a percentage – which is an easier number to understand and compare (Figure 7.7).

The costs we might include in a social media ROI calculation are:

- Internal resources (e.g. overheads, management time).
- External resources (e.g. graphic design, copywriting).
- Social media management tools (e.g. Hootsuite).
- Advertising costs (e.g. sponsoring content on LinkedIn, running a promoted Tweet or boosting a Facebook post).

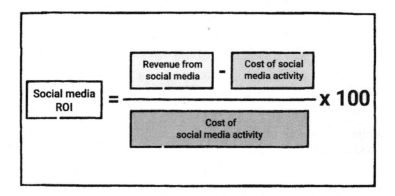

Figure 7.7. How to calculate social media ROI.

At its simplest, a social media ROI calculation could be completed for a specific campaign using Google Analytics and sales data. For example:

- 1,000 clicks from ten social media campaign posts on Twitter.
- Of those 1,000 clicks, 500 converted to a lead by filling in a form on a website landing page.
- Of those 500 leads, 100 ended up making a purchase.
- This means our traffic-to-lead conversion ratio is 50%, and our lead-to-sale conversion ratio is 20%.
- We know each purchase generates £100 in revenue and £500 of resources were allocated to the ten campaign posts.
- The campaign generated £10,000 of revenue (100 customers × £100) and £9,500 in profit (£10,000 – £500).

- The ROI is 19:1 (for every £1 spent, £19 of profit was generated), or 1900%.

You may see measurements for the ROI of social media advertising called Return on Advertising Spend (ROAS). It's the same calculation.

However, ROI/ROAS calculations do not take into account the time you spend setting up profiles, building audiences and posting content focused on building awareness in readiness for the campaign. While these activities may not yield immediate revenue, they contribute to long-term brand recognition, customer trust and overall marketing effectiveness.

Sentiment analysis

So far, we've considered ways to count our target audience's activity in response to our social media posts. It's also important to understand how our social media messages are being received emotionally.

Sentiment analysis is a powerful technique used for organic social media measurement to analyse and understand the emotion behind social media posts, comments or reviews, diving deeper than reach, impressions and engagements. It involves the process of determining whether a piece of text expresses a positive, negative or neutral sentiment. An organisation launching a new product might use sentiment analysis to gauge customer reactions to that product, for example. And sentiment analysis could be used to track the effectiveness of PR efforts or to monitor brand reputation.

For example, you could monitor mentions, then categorise the feedback into positive, negative or neutral sentiment by looking for positive or negative words such as

- love, amazing, great, best (positive)
- bad, awful, terrible, fail (negative).

The challenge with sentiment analysis is context. For example, the word 'brilliant' may appear to be positive, but users are often sarcastic, and a post like 'My flight is delayed, brilliant' would be negative.

A quantitative analysis of sentiment would include reviewing scores over time. Qualitative analysis would look at the nuances of language and emotion.

You can find some sentiment analysis features within tools such as Hootsuite (www.hootsuite.com) and Sprout Social. Brandwatch (www.brandwatch.com) is also a useful tool to consider.

Additional resources

For more on Sentiment Analysis, I recommend *Sentiment Analysis: Mining Opinions, Sentiments and Emotions* by Bing Liu.

Share of voice

Complementary to sentiment analysis is share of voice (SOV). Share of voice refers to the proportion or percentage of the overall online conversation or discussion that a particular brand occupies within a specific market. It allows organisations to assess their presence and influence in comparison to competitors.

Measuring share of voice was key to the growth of ContentCal (our case study in Chapter 4), and positive sentiment was recognised as an important success factor.

Various measurements can be used to measure share of voice, including the number of mentions, social media engagement, reach and impressions. An increasing share of voice indicates that your brand is reaching and resonating with a larger audience.

Combined with sentiment analysis for context and tone, you can build a useful understanding of the overall perception of your brand. Mentionlytics (www.mentionlytics.com) is a powerful monitoring solution for social media sentiment and brand mentions.

Aligning social media measurements with the marketing funnel

Figure 7.8 shows how these social media measurements align with the marketing funnel. At the awareness stage, reach, impressions, video views and share of voice are most valuable. For the interest and desire stages, engagement video complete watches (i.e. to the end of the video, not just the first few seconds), website traffic, lead generation and sentiment analysis are important measurements. At the action stage, conversion is key.

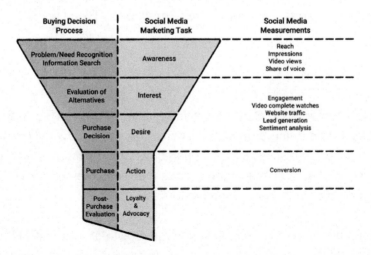

Figure 7.8. The marketing funnel and associated social media measurements.

From collecting data to finding actionable insights

The point of looking at social media measurements isn't just to prove that your social media activity has value, but so you can use the results to continually improve your activity and increase that value over time.

Imagine yourself as a rockstar standing before a large audience. The way the audience responds provides valuable data. When they are dancing and singing along, it indicates that they are loving your content. Conversely, if their arms are folded and they remain still, it signifies that they are not connecting with your performance. In response, you adapt your set list, aiming to keep them engaged and enthusiastic. This audience feedback serves as crucial information that shapes your future actions and decisions.

You need to take the same approach with social media data. We can call this structure 'start, stop, continue'.

To begin, the 'start' aspect involves identifying new tactics, or content ideas based on the insights gleaned from social media data. Analysing the data can help uncover trends, patterns, and audience preferences that can guide the creation of fresh content. For example, if certain types of posts consistently generate higher engagement rates or receive positive sentiment, you can consider starting to produce more of that content to capitalise on its success.

Next, the 'stop' element entails recognising and discontinuing ineffective or underperforming activities based on the data insights. By identifying posts that receive minimal engagement, negative sentiment, or fail to contribute to the desired outcomes, you can make informed decisions about ceasing those efforts.

Lastly, the 'continue' aspect involves acknowledging and nurturing successful practices identified through the data analysis. By identifying posts that consistently yield positive outcomes, you can continue leveraging those approaches to maintain or increase the value generated from your social media activity.

Recording of social media data should be ongoing and reviewed at regular intervals, perhaps monthly. Review this too infrequently and the information can build up and become too much to process, or you might miss opportunities. Review too often and you could invest a lot of effort without gaining any further benefit, or be tempted to act without having built up a true understanding of what's happening.

Analysing social media data can provide valuable insights to inform decision-making and create actions:

- Understanding reach and impressions help you to identify the visibility of your content and determine future opportunities for expanding brand awareness.
- Analysing engagement rates reveals which content resonates most with your audience, guiding future content planning.
- Measuring conversions such as actions taken when someone visits your website will help you maximise the impact of social media on overall online performance.
- Evaluating ROI enables organisations to assess campaign effectiveness and allocate future resources accordingly.
- Sentiment analysis helps gauge audience perception and address potential issues or areas for improvement.
- Measuring share of voice provides insights into brand visibility compared to competitors, influencing brand awareness initiatives and key messaging.

Testing

Since social media changes frequently, what works well today might very well change next month, so you need to keep testing and keep measuring.

Testing allows you to experiment with different tactics, content types, targeting approaches, and messaging to optimise your results. It involves systematically making one change at a time and measuring the impact of that change.

To conduct effective testing in social media marketing, it's important to establish clear objectives and define the specific variables you want to test. These variables can include elements like ad copy, imagery, targeting options, call-to-action buttons, budget, posting times, or even different social media platforms. By isolating one variable at a time, you can accurately assess its impact on your desired metrics and draw actionable conclusions.

When conducting tests, it's crucial to measure and track the results meticulously. This involves closely monitoring relevant measurements such as engagement rates, click-through rates, conversions, or any other key indicators that align with your goals and objectives. Use platform-specific insights or third-party tools to gather the necessary data and evaluate the performance of each test variation.

Sharing your results

While you are using data and insights to improve the performance of your social media marketing, it's likely that you will need to share your results with stakeholders across the organisation. If you are not asked to do this, you should proactively offer the information!

We asked in our research if marketers had difficulty telling others about the results of their social media marketing. Reassuringly (as shown in Figure 7.9), in 2020, 79% of respondents agreed that they would have no difficulty and in 2022 the response was 84.3%. Phew!

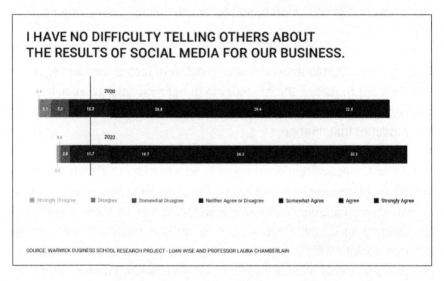

Figure 7.9. Responses to the statement, 'I have no difficulty telling others about the results of social media

As part of the 2020 and 2022 qualitative research interviews, we explored the topic of presenting social media measurements to the board. There was some frustration in this, as highlighted in the quotes below:

> Social media is just a thing you do.
> The board doesn't recognise the thought process that goes behind it.

> There's only a smattering of people in the business that appreciate the work we do on social media.

If it's something the board doesn't necessarily understand, it can be tricky to get budget approval.

We learned that when board members don't understand social media (most often when they don't use it themselves), they may be dissatisfied over the timelines involved (it taking longer to get results than they expect) with boards tending to look at revenue coming in now (short term) rather than assessing ROI over the longer term. This lack of understanding of timelines (how long it takes to see results) has led some organisations to regard social media as an expense, not an investment, and some have put their social media budgets on hold and reduced levels of activity. Others simply wanted visibility (with no input on what to post).

Can you make my Twitter feed look busy?

Another research participant commented that gaining board buy-in for social media campaigns was easier if they could equate the social media platform with traditional marketing models. For example, a Facebook ad, which consists of a picture and some text, is like an advertisement in a magazine. The participant also remarked that they knew their board members did not understand social media and were not interested in the thinking that went into it; so, when reporting to the board, they benchmarked their results against their competitors and provided broader insights, which were received more positively. Providing information in a context like this helps people understand it more easily.

Benchmarks

Benchmarks refer to reference points or standards that help evaluate performance and measure progress in comparison to established norms or competitors.

In Chapter 4 we looked at some options for analysing competitors' social media presence and activity; this is valuable data for benchmarking and understanding how you compare to others in your industry.
Many reports and tools provide aggregated data on social media trends, audience behaviour, and engagement rates for benchmarking. My go-to resources are DataReportal (www.datareportal.com) and Socialinsider (www.socialinsider.io). Although extremely useful in offering guidance, it is important to recognise that research reports are not specific to your organisation; the data is consolidated from various sources and may include data from multiple industry sectors and locations for example.

It is more valuable to use your own data to set benchmarks and then seek to test and improve on the results over time.

Although proving the value of social media marketing to a board that largely does not use it is problematic, another problem is that marketers are poor at marketing themselves. In her book *Marketing in the Boardroom: Winning the Hearts and Minds of the Board*, Ruth Saunders comments that marketers fail to market themselves adequately when presenting to the board.

For marketers to be heard in the boardroom, she says, they need to present strong recommendations; think and talk like the board, demonstrate how their proposed strategy will be profitable and engage the board in problem-solving.

When you're deciding what to measure and why, spend time considering how you will present these measurements and what they will mean to the board. Be bold, be confident, and remember that the board are a key stakeholder in communications: speak to them using words, images and values that resonate with them. For example, with your finance director, talk ROI. With a sales director, talk lead generation.

You may find that you need to educate your board about social media measurement. They may not be familiar with the data that's available, or even the terminology. This can create internal barriers and so the time taken to understand the data and insights that would be of interest and value to the board is key for all parties involved to feel both valued and understood.

Chapter summary

In this chapter, we have focused on understanding which social media measurements matter most to our organisation.

As social media marketers, we can use data to measure and continually improve the effectiveness of our activities. A 'start, stop, continue' structure is helpful to this approach. In the ever-changing world of social media, ongoing testing is essential.

Finally, we need to get better at communicating what we do internally. If we recognise the extent to which others within the organisation, including board members, understand social media, we can tailor our reports and conversations to their needs, and be heard.

Actions

- Ensure that you know how to find the measurements that matter to your organisation via your social media accounts, Google Analytics and any other tools you might have (such as a CRM system).
- Download an up-to-date *Guide to Native Social Media Analytics* (including how to set key performance indicators and a reporting template) by visiting by my website at www.luanwise.co.uk/books/planning-for-success/social-media-analytics or scanning the QR code below.
- On a regular basis (at least monthly), review your data using the 'start, stop, continue' approach.
- Conduct testing to experiment with different tactics, content types, targeting approaches and messaging to continually improve results.
- Consider how you will present your results to your colleagues, speaking their language, and communicating the value of social media as an investment.
- There is space to include the measurements that matter to your business on your one-page social media marketing plan.

Chapter 8

Balancing the benefits and risks of social media

In this chapter, we will:

- Recognise some key fears associated with social media and how we might overcome them.
- Understand the requirement for a social media policy to cover potential risks, and what it should include.
- Learn how to manage customers' day-to-day concerns and be prepared for a crisis if a situation escalates.

You may now have a completed one-page social media marketing plan, but let's pause for a moment before diving into action. While the plan sets the foundation for success, it's equally important to consider potential risks and be prepared to minimise their impact.

Social media has become such an integral part of our lives, both personal and professional. For individuals, it's a way to connect with friends and family, discover new brands and to be entertained. For organisations, it can be used to guide potential customers through the buying decision process, and towards loyalty and advocacy.

Social media provides us with real-time opportunities to understand the world around us and engage with others – friends, family, peers and colleagues. There are no boundaries of time or distance.

However, despite all its benefits, it is crucial that we do not overlook the fears and risks associated with social media use, both for individuals and organisations.

Fighting the fear of social media

In Chapter 3 we learned that there are often fears around the use of technology, and how this can be a barrier to using social media for work.

During my consultancy and training work, I hear many concerns and fears; these are the most common:

- **Fear of negative feedback or criticism:** People may be hesitant to engage on social media because they fear negative comments or criticism from customers, competitors, or others. This fear may be amplified by the viral nature of social media, where a single negative comment can quickly spread and damage a brand's reputation.
- **Fear of being perceived as unprofessional or inappropriate:** People worry that their social media presence will not be seen as professional or may contain content that is inappropriate for their target audience. This fear may be particularly strong for those in industries with more conservative or traditional reputations. Some digital immigrants share that they feel 'too old' to be active on social media platforms.
- **Fear of time and resource constraints:** Building a strong social media presence can be time-consuming and may require significant resources, both in terms of time and

financial investment. People may be hesitant to commit to social media because they feel they lack the time or resources to do it effectively and consistently.

- **Fear of the unknown:** social media changes so frequently, even experienced social media managers fear the unknown such as the launch of a new platform, or using a new feature for the first time.

I acknowledge all these as legitimate concerns, and it's important not to dismiss them. However, by gaining a better understanding of social media platforms, actively using them, and receiving proper training, many of these fears can be addressed.

In social media marketing, we're all still learning. And that's OK. I love this quote (source unknown) shared during our qualitative research:

In social media, you go to bed an expert and wake up a novice.

Reputation management

It is useful to explore the intertwined nature of managing personal and organisational brand reputation.

Most activity on LinkedIn is via individuals using their personal profiles to build networks and nurture relationships. While organisations may manage brand-led accounts, very often individuals will be representing themselves – for example, on Twitter, or interacting in Facebook Groups via their personal page. What individuals post on social media can have a direct impact not only on their personal brand but also on their employers' reputation.

Managing brand reputation – whether personal or brand-led – is critical. The social media listening tools we discussed for competitor research in Chapter 4 are helpful here (Semrush, Google Alerts,

Twitter Lists). We can monitor mentions of social media accounts and keywords (including names and hashtags), and use sentiment analysis to provide us with real-time insights. This helps us to take action in a timely fashion, should a problem occur.

In the same way that we take a planned approach, with clear content pillars to provide a framework for our day-to-day activity on social media, we need a planned approach to managing risk. Thinking in advance about how we will react to different scenarios allows us to think rationally, rather than reacting in the heat of the moment.

There are two stages to this: providing advice and direction to employees in the form of a social media policy and training and having a crisis management plan in place.

Social media policy

A social media policy should provide employees representing an organisation on social media, either using corporate accounts or via their own personal profiles with guidelines on what to do – and what not to do.

Problems that can occur include defamation, discrimination, obscenity, harassment, data protection issues (GDPR), trade descriptions issues, IP rights, brand reputation and the confidentiality of sensitive business information. These are not issues unique to social media. Therefore, a social media policy might be part of an internet use policy, and may also reference other policies, such as confidentiality, diversity, and equal opportunities.

The purpose of the social media policy should be empowering, rather than restrictive. It should provide reassurance and confidence to those who are using social media while shedding light on areas to consider.

Whether you need to start from scratch or whether you have an existing social media policy to review, I recommend a roundtable discussion that includes representatives from different teams, including HR and marketing.

There will be nuances involved in the discussion, and the more examples you can give when you share the policy, the better. Discuss dos as well as don'ts. When looking at content-sharing, you can give a framework for what might you share, what resources are suitable, and which ones are not suitable.

Guidelines in a social media policy are likely to be set around:

- Target response times to queries.
- Working hours/out-of-hours activity.
- Negative comments about the organisation or its employees.
- Comments that might be considered offensive (on protected characteristics such as sex, race, religion, or sexual orientation).
- Handling and reporting inappropriate content.
- Recording and reporting information.
- How/where to obtain further information or advice.
- Consequences of breaching social media policy and how the disciplinary process will operate.

It is a good idea to ask a solicitor to check your social media policy to ensure your organisation is adequately protected from liability. All employees should be asked to read the policy (and sign a document to that end) when it is introduced; it should also be part of the induction process for new employees.

As an individual posting on social media, I also recommend preparing your own 'social media dos and don'ts' guidelines. This will help you maintain your personal brand and thought leadership goals and objectives.

Social media and personal data

In the UK, the good news as far as consent and data use are concerned, when it comes to the General Data Protection Regulation (GDPR) and social media, they are effectively covered by the terms and conditions and privacy notices of each of the social media platforms.

The area for caution when it comes to social media and GDPR is extracting personal data from a platform and storing it within your organisation. For example, it is only acceptable to take an email address from social media, hold it on a CRM system or use it in any email marketing activity if you can justify doing so via one of the six legal grounds (consent, performance of a contract, a legitimate interest, a vital interest, a legal requirement or a public interest), and provided you comply with the data protection principles. It's not impossible, but it can be quite tricky to achieve.

You can continue to message users via the social media platform where you have made a connection, but you can't move the communication to any other marketing channel unless you can satisfy those legal grounds and comply with the data protection principles.

If you are providing personal data to a social media platform for advertising purposes, for example in the form of an email list for building custom audiences, you will need to have the right permissions.

For more information, visit www.ico.org.uk/for-organisations/guide-to-data-protection/guide-to-the-general-data-protection-regulation-gdpr/.

Use of artificial intelligence (AI)

The use of artificial intelligence tools is increasing, and you might wish to consider incorporating how you will use AI into your social media policy.

AI tools are being used to support social media content creation, and social media platforms are now incorporating AI-powered features, for example, a premium LinkedIn account user can access AI support in writing their profile and in writing job listings.

At the time of writing, it is still very early days and its application is constantly evolving. There is great potential in using AI to achieve social media marketing goals more efficiently, however, there are concerns around data privacy and also ethical considerations. I'm sure that the monthly update webinars I co-host with Andy Lambert will cover this topic regularly, so don't forget to join us (details are listed at www.thelighthouse.social/events).

Handling negative situations on social media

Customers often turn to social media to voice their frustrations or concerns. According to research by Khoros, almost 50% of the engagement intent of social media users is related to customer care. It's therefore essential that the 'front line' of your organisation, i.e. your social media managers, are ready and able to respond.

The Khoros research also showed that customers expect to receive a response to their query within three hours.

For brands who do meet customers' expectations in response to messages and posts involving complaints, customer loyalty is often enhanced – customers continue to give their business to the brand

179

and become more receptive to a brand's advertisements, encouraging friends and family to buy a brand's products or use their services, and even praising or recommending the brand on social media.

However, if negative messages are not addressed in a timely and effective manner, they can escalate.

Case study: Turning a crisis into positive PR

In February 2018, Kentucky Fried Chicken (KFC), a popular global fast-food chain, faced a major crisis in the UK when it experienced a shortage of chicken, a core ingredient in its menu items.

This resulted in the temporary closure of over two-thirds of their outlets across the UK, leading to significant negative media coverage and public backlash. The crisis threatened to tarnish KFC's reputation and brand image.

Recognising the urgency to address the crisis and take control of the narrative, KFC responded swiftly with a proactive and authentic approach.

Within days of the store closures, they published a full-page advertisement in several prominent UK newspapers, featuring an image of a KFC bucket with letters rearranged to spell 'FCK'. The headline read, "We're sorry. A chicken restaurant without any chicken. It's not ideal." The advertisement was accompanied by a heartfelt and candid apology, acknowledging their mistake, and taking responsibility for the inconvenience caused.
The campaign quickly went viral on social media, generating extensive media coverage and sparking a positive response from the public. KFC's approach garnered widespread praise

---

for its transparency, humour, and humility. The FCK campaign effectively conveyed that KFC understood the severity of the situation and empathised with its customers.

The campaign not only diffused negative sentiment but also generated significant positive publicity and customer support. The apology and honest response resonated with the public, leading to increased brand loyalty and improved perception of KFC as a responsible and customer-centric organisation.

When an issue escalates

By promoting responsible social media use and setting clear expectations for employees, an organisation can reduce the risk of incidents. However, it is more difficult to keep control over external events and other users.

The Institute for Public Relations (www.instituteforpr.org) defines a crisis as:

A significant threat to operations that can have negative consequences if not handled properly. In crisis management, the threat is the potential damage a crisis can inflict on an organisation, its stakeholders, and an industry. A crisis can create three related threats: (1) public safety, (2) financial loss, and (3) reputation loss. Some crises, such as industrial accidents and product harm, can result in injuries and even loss of lives. Crises can create financial loss by disrupting operations, creating a loss of market share/purchase intentions, or spawning lawsuits related to the crisis.

Often a crisis situation starts away from social media but quickly appears online as it is the perfect channel for real-time communication, and social media managers then find themselves involved. An increased number of mentions and messages on social media is an early indication that something is starting to escalate.

While the social media team might be heavily involved in managing messages and social media listening, crisis management should involve other team members, such as HR and senior leadership. There are different roles – such as writing content and monitoring comments. Please do not leave this to one person or take this on by yourself.

Crisis management planning

In 2020, 25% of our research respondents agreed that they did not know what to do if something on social media went wrong; 14.1% neither agreed nor disagreed. In 2022, 30.9% agreed that they did not know what to do if things went wrong, and 16.9% neither agreed nor disagreed. These results are shown in Figure 8.1.

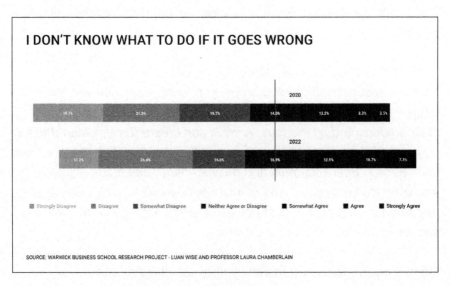

Figure 8.1. Responses to the statement, 'I don't know what to do if it [social media] goes wrong.'

Within your organisation, you need to have a crisis management plan ready and waiting. Potential risks should be included within your social media policy so that all employees can be aware and able to help identify potential situations should they arise.

A framework for crisis management

One recognised framework for crisis management is HEARD: it's an acronym for Hear, Evaluate, Act, Reassure and Debrief.

Here is a brief summary of each step:

Hear

The first step in the HEARD approach is to listen carefully to what is being said about the crisis, both internally and externally. This involves monitoring social media, news reports and other sources of information to gain a full understanding of what's happening. At this stage, a quick decision should be made about social media content that has been scheduled. It may be prudent to pause posts as soon as possible. A mistimed scheduled post can cause offence and add fire to an emerging situation.

Evaluate

Once you have gathered more information about the crisis, the next step is to evaluate the situation. A RAG rating is a traffic light rating system often used to assess the severity of a crisis and determine an appropriate response. RAG stands for Red, Amber, and Green.

A RAG rating of red indicates a severe crisis that requires immediate attention, while amber represents a crisis that is significant but not as urgent, and green represents a situation that is under control or not significant. By using a RAG rating system, a crisis management team

Luan Wise

can prioritise their response efforts and allocate resources accordingly, ensuring that they are effectively addressing the most urgent issues first.

Here are some areas you could include:

- what is being said – the seriousness of the issue
- who is saying it – the influence or authority of the person who posts it (this can have a knock-on effect on others' perceptions of the issue)
- frequency – is the issue getting more visible, or less?

Act

The third step in the HEARD approach is to take action to address the crisis. The 'golden first hour' is key, and your brand needs to own the response by being the first to respond (before someone else takes ownership of the narrative).

During the crisis, everything should be documented. Take screenshots of every social media post, keep copies of emails sent, internal meeting notes, and more. These will be important records for the debrief and future planning.

During busy periods, such as a crisis, you might find utilising auto-responders on social media accounts is beneficial for managing customer expectations and providing efficient communication. These automated messages acknowledge customer enquiries, indicating when they can expect a response or where to find relevant information in the meantime. For this, regular update posts are valuable and these should be pinned to the top of your profiles.

Reassure

The fourth step is to reassure stakeholders that you are taking the situation seriously and are committed to resolving the crisis. The sooner you can acknowledge a situation, the better. You can use a simple holding pattern of responses starting with information such as 'We're aware of the current situation. Please be assured that we're looking into it and will share more information as soon as we have it.' You should then provide regular updates and communicate in a transparent and empathetic manner, while continuing to monitor. Proactive posts on social media accounts will help you manage individual messages coming into your inboxes.

Debrief

The final step in the HEARD approach is to debrief and evaluate the crisis response. This involves reviewing what worked well and what could be improved, and incorporating lessons learned into future crisis management planning.

Do you remember doing regular fire drills at school? A practice run of your crisis management plan is also advisable.

As your crisis situation comes to an end, consider when it is appropriate to return to your 'business-as-usual' activity and if there are any sensitivities that might need to be considered when preparing future content.

Case study: The Met Office: Using social media to keep the UK safe in a crisis

The Met Office is funded by the government to provide a national weather service for all citizens of the UK. A critical part of the Met Office's remit is to provide information that will help people take appropriate decisions/actions to stay safe, particularly during severe weather.

In February 2022, the UK experienced an unprecedented event: three severe storms within a week. Six days before the first storm, the Met Office started a new campaign to raise awareness. It utilised organic and paid content tailored to each social media channel's strengths, shaping the news agenda by using storm name hashtags, with the aim of establishing the Met Office as the authoritative source for accurate updates during the crisis, countering fake news – rife in the weather sector. TikTok, Twitter and YouTube played key roles in reaching different groups through presenter-led quick forecasts, real-time safety updates on Twitter Spaces, and longer-form content discussing uncertainties and impacts on YouTube.

Partnerships directly with the social media platforms and organisations such as the Royal National Lifeboat Institution (RNLI) helped to further amplify the Met Office's content and reach new audiences with important safety messages.

By effectively communicating weather information, providing timely updates and encouraging appropriate action, the Met Office achieved high public awareness of storm impacts and warnings, with 97–98% awareness and 87% of surveyed individuals taking action.

Its social media campaign exceeded all expectations, gaining the Met Office 125,500 followers, including 47,000 new followers on TikTok, and generating millions of video views. Most importantly, the information it shared influenced and motivated audiences to take action, such as changing their travel plans and staying inside.

Thanks to Met Office Creative Lead Ross Middleham for sharing this case study.

You can follow the Met Office on social media: @metoffice

Chapter summary

In this final chapter, we balance the many benefits of social media we've learned about throughout this book with understanding common fears and some potential pitfalls. By following our clear thinking and planned approach to using social media, you can be well prepared to identify and manage day-to-day issues and potential crises by preparing a social media policy and having a crisis management plan in place.

Actions

- Review your social media policy. If you do not have a social media policy for your organisation, you should consult with colleagues to prepare one. Write it clearly, and include examples of good and bad practices. If you are actively managing your personal brand on social media, consider your own dos and don'ts and ensure that they align with those of your employer.

- Build your crisis management team and meet regularly to discuss risks and update your crisis management plan.

Summary of actions

Congratulations! You have made it to the final summary of actions. I know there's a lot to do – and keep doing – to achieve your desired social media marketing goals, but it is all achievable.

Take your time – there is no need to rush. Keep revisiting this book whenever you need to.

While I have guided you through the stages of the planning process, I have chosen to omit sample social media marketing plans from this book. Your business, goals and audience are unique to you. I have equipped you with a tried-and-tested framework and suggested actions: now it's up to you to prepare your plan.

However, if you would like some support, I'm always here to help. I never say no to a coffee… I invite you to visit my website at www.luanwise.co.uk to see how we might work together.

Here's a reminder of the one-page social media marketing plan template, and where you can find the information within the book:

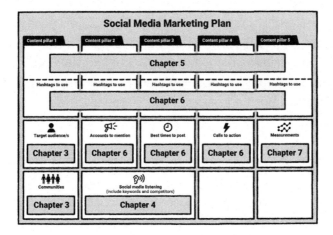

The template and links to all website pages listed below can be accessed by visiting my website at www.luanwise.co.uk/books/ planning-for-success/one-page-plan or by scanning the QR code below.

Chapter 1: Understanding the ever-changing social media landscape

- Visit www.thelighthouse.social to subscribe to email updates for the latest news and event information.
- Reviewing industry award winners provides valuable insights into successful approaches. You might also consider entering your own campaigns for awards! Look at the B2B Marketing Awards (https://events.b2bmarketing.net/b2bawards), Chartered Institute of Marketing Excellence Awards (https://www.cim.co.uk/global-marketing-excellence-awards/), Chartered Institute of Public Relations Excellence Awards (www.cipr.co.uk), The Drum Social Buzz Awards (www.thedrumawards.com) and the Global and UK Social Media Awards (https://dontpanicprojects.com/our-awards/). A full list of UK business awards can be found at www.awards-list.co.uk.

Chapter 2: Setting meaningful social media goals and objectives

- Make sure you have access to your business plan so that you understand your organisation's vision, mission and 'big picture' view.

- Watch Simon Sinek's TED Talk, 'Start with Why' on YouTube. Visit www.simonsinek.com for his books – including Start with *Why* and *Find your Why* and other resources – to help find your own purpose.
- When setting objectives, ensure that you include all five SMART criteria – specific, measurable, achievable, relevant and time-bound.

Chapter 3: Defining your target audience

- For each of your products and services, write down the problems you solve for your customers.
- Be clear about how your market is segmented, and which audience/s your organisation is focused on targeting.
- Understand who might be involved in the buying decision process, and which roles within the decision-making unit you might need to address and prioritise for social media marketing.
- Revisit existing customer personas or start afresh using the persona generator by visiting www.luanwise.co.uk/books/planning-for-success/persona-generator or by scanning the QR code below. There is space to include the names of your personas on the one-page social media marketing plan template.
- Follow your target audience on different social media platforms. This includes your current customers, and also potential customers.
- Which groups/communities are you currently participating in? Review the list to check that they are still relevant and useful to you. Do some research on new communities you might join. List them on your one-page social media marketing plan.

Chapter 4: Examining the social media competition

- List your direct and indirect competitors.
- Create a list of the social media platforms they are using, and their account details.
- Start to follow your competitors, either via your own organisation accounts, or a personal account.
- Set up a template document, perhaps in Microsoft Excel and/or Powerpoint to capture relevant competitor insights.
- Use the following questions to review your competitors' accounts. Add any additional questions relevant to your own organisation, products and services.
  - How many followers do they have?
  - How often do they post content?
  - What content formats are they using?
  - What posts do they have pinned?
  - What 'Highlight' categories are they using on Instagram?
  - What hashtags are they using?
  - Do they include a branded hashtag that you could follow?
  - Who is engaging with their content?
  - What kind of content do their audiences engage with most/least?
  - What comments do their audiences leave?
  - How does the organisation respond to comments?
- Look at your competitors' advertising activity. Note what products and services they are promoting and what creative options they might be testing.
- Review potential tools for social monitoring and identify relevant keywords and topics that you could track. Possible tools include Google Alerts, Twitter Lists, Brandwatch and Talkwalker.

- Search for relevant groups, for example on Facebook and LinkedIn, where you can engage in social research and helpful conversations with your target audiences.
- Make an informed decision about the social media platforms you will start using for your organisation by asking:
    - What do you want to achieve?
    - Who is your target audience? What social media platforms are they using?
    - What platforms are your competitors using? How do they use them?
    - What resources do you have available?
- Ensure you have internal processes in place to share competitor and audience insights with your colleagues and relevant external partners (eg agencies/freelancers).

Chapter 5: Creating a social media content calendar

- Decide on your content pillars and add them to your one-page social media marketing plan template.
- Create a 12-month content calendar. Do some research using a website such as www.daysoftheyear.com, www.onthisday.com and www.thisdayinmusic.com and add key dates relevant to your organisation.
- Create a content inventory spreadsheet. Ensure you keep the inventory up to date: you could add a recurring appointment to your calendar as a reminder to you to check it.
- Build monthly and weekly calendars, as required. You could use an Excel spreadsheet, online planning tools such as Asana (www.asana.com), Trello (www.trello.com) or Monday.com (www.monday.com), or the calendar feature in a social media management tool such as Hootsuite or Sprout Social.
- Look at each social media platform you have chosen to use, and ensure that you know how to find trending content there.

- Decide how you will curate content to share on social media. Set up Google Alerts, subscribe to an RSS feed, create some Twitter lists or whichever methods work for you.
- Make sure you have notifications switched on for mentions of your social media accounts so that you can look out for user-generated content.

Chapter 6: Maximising your social media marketing efforts

- Diarise a recurring appointment to review your account set-ups (perhaps quarterly).
- If you do not have brand or tone of voice guidelines, review the example from Monzo. You will find other examples if you search online. Check that any existing guidelines include information about social media content.
- Do some hashtag research for each of your content pillars. Use tools such as hashtags.org, hashtagify.me, best-hashtags.com or the app Tagomatic. Add the list of hashtags to your one-page social media marketing plan, and save them in a Notes file or a Word file for easy access when you are posting content.
- Look through your social media accounts to identify where you can implement best practices, including a consistent visual style, correct image sizing, and tailoring for each platform. How inclusive and accessible is your content? Try experiencing your social media posts via a screen reader, watching videos with your eyes closed, and using a colour contrast checker to review your images.
- Add a list of relevant calls to action to your one-page social media marketing plan.
- Look at your social media account insights to discover when your audience is most active. Add to your one-page social media marketing plan the best times to post. If you do not

have account insights, search for industry reports and set out a plan to test what works best for you.

- Review your website. Start with checking technical issues, such as broken links and site speed. Then put yourselves in your customer's shoes and see how easy your site is to navigate. Can you find the information you want to find? Referring back to your content inventory will help with this exercise.
- Create a list of individuals and organisations you might mention in your social media posts. Add the usernames to your one-page social media marketing plan.
- Consider how you might involve your colleagues with social media. Could you set up an employee advocacy programme?
- Who might you collaborate with? Are influencers right for your organisation? Schedule some time to research potential partnerships and create an action plan to explore potential opportunities.

Chapter 7: Understanding the measurements that matter

- Ensure that you know how to find the measurements that matter to your organisation via your social media accounts, Google Analytics and any other tools you might have (such as a CRM system).
- Download an up-to-date *Guide to Native Social Media Analytics* guide (including how to set key performance indicators and a reporting template) by visiting by my website at www.luanwise.co.uk/books/planning-for-success/social-media-analytics.
- On a regular basis (at least monthly), review your data using the 'start, stop, continue' approach.

- Conduct testing to experiment with different tactics, content types, targeting approaches and messaging to continually improve results.
- Consider how you will present your results to your colleagues, speaking their language, and communicating the value of social media as an investment.
- There is space to include the measurements that matter to your business on your one-page social media marketing plan.

Chapter 8: Balancing the benefits and risks of social media

- Review your social media policy. If you do not have a social media policy for your organisation, you should consult with colleagues to prepare one. Write it clearly, and include examples of good and bad practices. If you are actively managing your personal brand on social media, consider your own dos and don'ts and ensure that they align with those of your employer.
- Build your crisis management team and meet regularly to discuss risks and update your crisis management plan.

Glossary

Accessibility: The practice of designing and developing social media content and posts that provide a smooth, inclusive experience for everyone.

AIDA: A marketing model by Edward Kellogg Strong Jr (1925) representing stages of the marketing task. An acronym for Attention, Interest, Desire, and Action.

Algorithm: The complex set of rules and calculations used by social media platforms to determine the content that users see on their feeds.

Awareness: The state of recognising or understanding a particular concept, idea, product, or brand.

BeReal: A social media app released in 2020, developed by Alexis Barreyat and Kévin Perreau. Its main feature is a daily notification that encourages users to share a photo of themselves and their immediate surroundings given a randomly selected two-minute window every day.

Benchmark: Reference points or standards that help evaluate performance and measure progress in comparison to established norms or competitors.

Boomer: Informal term referring to a member of the baby boomer generation, typically born between the mid-1940s and mid-1960s.

Buying decision process: The series of steps an individual goes through before making a purchase, including problem/need recognition, information search, evaluation of alternatives, purchase decision, and post-purchase evaluation.

Bytedance: The Chinese tech company known for creating popular social media platforms like TikTok and Douyin.

Call to action: A prompt or instruction encouraging the audience to take a specific action.

Clubhouse: An audio-only app, launched in 2020, that allows users to participate in live discussions and conversations.

Collab post: A collaborative post created by multiple individuals or content creators working together on a single piece of content.

Community: A group of individuals sharing common interests, goals, or values, often engaging in discussions and interactions.

Community management: The process of engaging audiences across social media platforms to increase brand loyalty and grow authentic connections.

Competitor: A business, product, or individual contending with others for market share, attention, or resources. Competitors can be direct (offering similar products or services and targeting the same audience) or indirect (targeting the same audience but offering different products or services).

Content curation: The process of discovering, selecting, and sharing relevant and valuable content from various sources to engage an audience.

Content pillars: The core themes or topics that guide content for an organisation or individual.

Conversion: The desired action that a user or customer takes in response to a call to action, such as making a purchase, signing up, or subscribing.

Creator: An individual who produces and shares original content across various mediums, often online and on social media platforms.

Crisis management: The strategic process of handling and mitigating negative situations or events that could harm a brand's reputation or operations.

Customer persona: A reflection of your ideal target customer based on research and data. It is a detailed profile that includes your customer's demographic information, motivations, preferences and behaviours. Also known as a buyer persona or ideal customer portrait.

Deciders: The people who have the final say in the buying decision. Deciders usually rely on advice from other members of the decision-making unit and are influenced strongly by gatekeepers.

Decision-making unit (DMU): A collection or team of individuals who participate in a buyer *decision process*.

Differentiation: The process of establishing a unique and compelling identity for a product, service, or brand that sets it apart from competitors in the mind of its customers.

Digital immigrant: A person who grew up before the digital age and learned to use technology later in life.

Digital native: A person who has grown up using digital technology from an early age and is comfortable with its use.

Direct competitor: A business that offers similar products or services and competes directly for the same target audience.

Emoji: A small digital image or icon used to express emotions, ideas, or concepts in electronic communication.

Employee advocacy: The promotion of a company's brand, products or services by its employees through social media and other online channels.

Engagement: How people interact with your content. It's a measure for the 'social' part of social media and can include likes, shares, link clicks, mentions, comments, replies, direct (private) messages and video completions (watching a video to the end).

Ephemeral: messages and media that disappear after being viewed. For example, Instagram Stories that disappear 24 hours after being posted.

Ethnography: the practice of observing people in their own environment to understand their experiences, perspectives and everyday practices.

Evergreen content: Content that remains relevant and valuable to audiences over an extended period.

Facebook: A social media platform that connects people, allows sharing of content and facilitates social interactions.

Facebook Group: A community space on Facebook where users with common interests can share content, engage in discussions, and connect.

Filter: A digital tool used to modify or enhance images by applying visual effects or adjustments.

Focus group: A small group of individuals assembled to provide feedback and opinions on a product, service, or concept.

FOMO (Fear of Missing Out): The feeling of anxiety or apprehension that one might be missing out on interesting or exciting experiences.

Gatekeeper: Those who control the flow of information to others. They may be asked to collect information and/or to filter what information gets through to other members of the decision-making unit.

Generation Alpha: The generation born after Generation Z, typically starting from 2012 onwards.

Generation X: The generation born between the mid-1960s and 1980.

Generation Z: The generation born from the mid-1990s to early 2010s.

Goal: The broad, overarching statements that define the desired outcome of your social media marketing efforts. They provide a sense of direction and purpose for your activity. Goals are typically long-term and focus on the big picture.

Google Alert: A notification service that sends alerts when new content related to specific keywords is indexed by Google.

Google Analytics: A web analytics tool by Google that provides insights into website traffic and user behaviour.

Google+: A former social media platform by Google aimed at facilitating social interactions and content sharing.

Hashtag: A word or phrase preceded by the '#' symbol used to categorise and discover content on social media platforms.

Impressions: The number of times a piece of content is displayed to users, regardless of whether it's clicked or engaged with.

Indirect competitor: A business that offers different products or services but still competes for the same target audience.

Influencer: those who can influence the buying. They may include paid advisors and consultants external to the organisation. They can also include friends and family members.

Influencer: An individual with a significant online presence who can influence the opinions and behaviours of their followers

Initiators: are the people who first identify the problem/need for buying a particular product or service.

Instagram: A photo and video-sharing social media platform known for its visual-centric nature.

Lead generation: The process of identifying and capturing potential customers or leads who have shown interest in a product, service or brand.

LinkedIn: A professional networking platform that allows users to connect with colleagues, peers, and professionals in various industries.

LinkedIn company Page: A business profile on LinkedIn used to showcase company information, updates, and opportunities.

LinkedIn profile: An individual's professional profile on LinkedIn, highlighting their skills, experience, and connections.

Market segmentation: The process of dividing the total market for a good or service into several segments, each of which tends to be homogenous in all significant aspects with others within the segment, and heterogeneous from those in other segments.

Marketing funnel: A visual representation of the customer journey, from awareness to post-purchase evaluation.

Mention: A reference to a user, brand, or topic on social media.

Metaverse: A virtual-reality space in which users can interact with a computer-generated environment and other users.

Millennial: The generation born from the early 1980s to the mid-1990s.

Organic social media: Content and interactions that occur on social media platforms without any paid promotion.

Paid social media: Spending money to promote content and reach a wider audience. It includes various advertising formats such as sponsored posts, display ads, and influencer collaborations.

Personal brand: The process of establishing and promoting an individual as a brand.

Positioning: The unique place a product, service, or brand occupies in the minds of consumers relative to competitors.

Qualitative: Data or research that involves non-numerical insights and focuses on understanding behaviour and opinions.

Quantitative: Data or research that involves numerical measurements and statistical analysis.

Reach: The total number of followers/connections who have the chance to see your posts at any given point in time.

Reel: A short-form video format on Instagram and Facebook for creating and sharing engaging content.

Repurposing content: Adapting existing content for use in different formats.

Reputation management: Practices to maintain and enhance a brand's positive image and address negative perceptions.

Retargeting: Showing advertisements to users who have previously interacted with a brand but did not convert.

Return on advertising spend (ROAS): How the effectiveness of advertising campaigns are measured - by comparing the amount spent to the revenue generated.

Return on investment (ROI): A performance measure that looks at the benefit (or return) of doing something.

RSS (feed/reader): Really Simple Syndication, a software application or online service that allows users to aggregate and organise content from multiple websites or sources into a single location.

Sentiment analysis: A technique used for organic social media measurement to analyse and understand the emotion behind social media posts, comments or reviews.

Share of voice: The proportion or percentage of the overall online conversation or discussion that a particular brand occupies within a specific market.

Shiny object syndrome: A term used to describe the tendency for people to be easily distracted by new, attractive ideas, tools or technologies, instead of focusing on what they have been working on or what they have already established as a goal.

Short-form video: Brief video content, typically lasting a few seconds to a couple of minutes.

SMART objectives: An acronym for Specific, Measurable, Achievable, Relevant, and Time-bound.

Snapchat: A multimedia messaging app known for its temporary content sharing and disappearing messages.

Social media: An umbrella term that defines the various activities that integrate technology, social interaction and the construction of words, video, and audio.

Social media listening: The process of identifying and assessing what is being said about an organisation, individual, product or brand on the internet, and the issues that affect it.

Social media policy: A document that provides employees representing an organisation on social media, either using corporate accounts or via their own personal profiles with guidelines on what to do – and what not to do.

Social proof: Evidence that other people have purchased and found value in your products and services.

Stakeholder: Individuals, groups or any party that has an interest in the outcomes of an organisation.

Story: A narrative or sequence of content often used on social media platforms to engage and connect with an audience.

Storytelling: The art of conveying a message or information through a narrative that captures the audience's attention and emotion.

Subject matter expert: An individual with specialised knowledge and expertise in a specific field or topic.

Tactics: Specific actions and methods used to execute a strategy and achieve goals and objectives.

Target market: The specific group of individuals (segments) that a product or service is intended to serve and appeal to.

Targeting: The process of tailoring content or advertisements to reach a specific audience based on demographics, interests, and behaviours.

The Golden Circle: A concept by Simon Sinek that emphasises starting with 'why' (purpose) before addressing 'how' and 'what'.

Third-party: External entities or sources not directly affiliated with a brand or organisation.

Threads: An online social media and social networking service operated by Meta. Launched July 2023.

TikTok: A social media platform focused on short-form video content, popular for its creative and entertaining videos.

Thought leadership: The practice of sharing innovative ideas, insights, and expertise within a specific industry or field. It involves establishing oneself as an authority and a trusted source of knowledge, contributing to industry discussions, and shaping the direction of conversations.

Tone of voice: The personality, style, and language you use in your marketing messages.

Touchpoint: Any interaction between a brand and its audience occurring throughout the buying decision process.

Trending content: Content that is currently popular and widely discussed on social media platforms.

Twitter: A microblogging platform where users share short messages known as Tweets.

Twitter Communities: Groups of Twitter users with shared interests and conversations.

Twitter List: A curated list of Twitter accounts organised by a specific theme or category.

Twitter Spaces: An audio-only feature on Twitter that allows users to host live voice conversations.

User-generated content: Any form of content, such as images, videos or reviews, that is created and shared voluntarily by individuals who are not employed or affiliated with a brand or organisation.

YouTube: A video-sharing platform where users can upload, share, and view videos.

References and further reading

Links to all website pages and resources listed below can be accessed by visiting www.luanwise.co.uk/book/planning-for-success or by scanning the QR code below:

This includes *LinkedIn Success: The Ultimate Guide to Perfecting Your Profile* and *Guide to Native Social Media Analytics.*

Awards

B2B Marketing Awards: https://events.b2bmarketing.net/b2bawards

Chartered Institute of Marketing Excellence Awards: https://www.cim.co.uk/global-marketing-excellence-awards/

Chartered Institute of Public Relations Excellence Awards: www.cipr.co.uk

The Drum Social Buzz Awards: www.thedrumawards.com

Global and UK Social Media Awards: https://dontpanicprojects.com/our-awards/

A full list of UK business awards can be found at www.awards-list. co.uk.

Books

Jerry Angrave (2020) *The Journey Mapping Playbook: A Practical Guide to Preparing, Facilitating and Unlocking the Value of Customer Journey Mapping*. De Gruyter.

Matthew Brennan (2020) *Attention Factory: The Story of TikTok and China's ByteDance*. Independently published.

Michelle Carvill and Ian MacRae (2020) *Myths of Social Media: Dismiss the Misconceptions and Use Social Media Effectively in Business*. Kogan Page.

Susan Chritton (2014) *Personal Branding for Dummies.* For Dummies. A Wiley Brand.

Damian Corbet (2021) *The Social CEO: How Social Media Can Make You A Stronger Leader.* Bloomsbury Business.

Stephen R. Covey (1989) *The 7 Habits of Highly Effective People*. Simon & Schuster.

James Engel, David Kollat and Roger Blackwell (1968) *Consumer Behavior*. Holt, Rinehart and Winston.

Sarah Frier (2021) *No Filter: The Inside Story of Instagram*. Random House Business.

Leigh Gallagher (2018) *The Airbnb Story: How to Disrupt an Industry, Make Billions of Dollars … and Plenty of Enemies*. Virgin Books.

Bernadette Jiwa (2014) *Marketing: A Love Story: How to Matter to Your Customers*. Independently published.

Bing Liu (2020) *Sentiment Analysis: Mining Opinions, Sentiments and Emotions.* Cambridge University Press

Steven Levy (2020) *Facebook: The Inside Story.* Blue Rider Press.

Donald Miller (2017) *Building a Story Brand*. HarperCollins.

Michael E. Porter (1998) *The Competitive Advantage: Creating and Sustaining Superior Performance.* NY: Free Press.

Adele Revella (2015) *Buyer Personas: How to Gain Insight Into Your Customer's Expectations, Align Your Marketing Strategies and Win More Business*. John Wiley & Sons.

Al Ries and Jack Trout (2001) *Positioning: The Battle for your Mind*. McGraw Hill.

Ruth Saunders (2017) *Marketing in the Boardroom: Winning the Hearts and Minds of the Board*. Routledge.

Simon Sinek (2009) *Start with Why: How Great Leaders Inspire Everyone to Take Action*. Penguin. www.simonsinek.com

Simon Sinek (2017) *Find your Why: A Practical Guide for Discovering Purpose For You and Your Team*. Penguin. www.simonsinek.com

Bryony Thomas (2020) *Watertight Marketing: The Proven Process for Seriously Scaleable Sales.* Human Business Thinking.

Jack Trout and Steve Rivkin (2008) *Differentiate or Die: Survival in our Era of Killer Competiton.* Wiley.

Richard M.S. Wilson and Colin Gilligan (1997) *Strategic Marketing Management: Planning, Implementation and Control.* Butterworth Heinemann.

Amy Woods (2019) *Content 10×: More Content, Less Time, Maximum Results.* Content 10× Media. www.content10x.com

Case studies

Cheltenham Borough Council on LinkedIn: https://www.linkedin.com/company/cheltenham-borough-council/

Dove Real Beauty: www.dove.com/uk/stories/campaigns.html

Hilton Brands: www.hilton.com/en/brands/

Guild: www.guild.co

Marketing Meet Up: www.marketingmeetup.com

Met Office: www.metoffice.gov.uk

Monzo's tone of voice guidelines: https://monzo.com/tone-of-voice/

Xero Award Win – Serial Killer Receipts: www.museaward.com/winner-info.php?id=224435

Data sources

DataReportal global digital insights: https://datareportal.com/

Keynote market research: https://www.marketresearch.com/

Mintel market research: http://www.mintel.com/

Office for National Statistics (UK): https://www.ons.gov.uk/

Overdrive Interactive social media map: https://www.ovrdrv.com/knowledge/social-media-map/

Social Insider: www.socialinsider.io

United Nations statistics division: https://unstats.un.org/home/nso_sites

Publications cited throughout the book

Aimia (2012) *Staring at the Sun: Identifying, Understanding and Influencing Social Media Users*: https://www.prnewswire.com/news-releases/aimia-study-makes-case-for-segmentation-driven-social-media-strategy-based-on-six-social-media-personas-155925865.html

Chartered Institute of Marketing (2022) *Impact of Marketing*: https://www.cim.co.uk/content-hub/thought-leadership/impact-of-marketing-2022-report-rebuilding-better-customer-experiences/

Deloitte (2021) *A Call for Accountability and Action. The Deloitte Global Millennial and Gen Z Survey*: https://www2.deloitte.com/content/dam/Deloitte/se/Documents/about-deloitte/2021-deloitte-global-millennial-survey-report.pdf

Bill Gates (1996) *Content is King*: http://web.archive.org/web/20010126005200/http://www.microsoft.com/billgates/columns/1996essay/essay960103.asp

Hootsuite (2023) *Social Media Trends*: https://www.hootsuite.com/en-gb/research/social-trends

HP Inc (2022) *Hybrid Work: Are We There Yet?:* https://h20195.www2.hp.com/v2/getpdf.aspx/4AA8-2370EEW.pdf

Khoros (2023) *Social Media Customer Service*: https://khoros.com/blog/social-media-customer-service-stats

LinkedIn. *The Official Guide to Employee Advocacy*: https://business.linkedin.com/content/dam/me/business/en-us/elevate/Resources/pdf/official-guide-to-employee-advocacy-ebook.pdf

Local IQ (2022) *What Happens in an Internet Minute*: https://localiq.com/blog/what-happens-in-an-internet-minute/

Marketo (2019) *Creating Epic Customer Experiences*: https://engage.marketo.com/Epic-Experiences-B2B-Marketing-Leaders.html

Michael E. Porter (1996) *What is Strategy?* Harvard Business Review: https://hbr.org/1996/11/what-is-strategy

Mark Prensky (2001) *Digital Natives, Digital Immigrants: Part 1*: https://www.emerald.com/insight/content/doi/10.1108/10748120110424816/full/html

Sprout Social (2023) *Content Benchmarks Report*: https://sproutsocial. com/insights/data/content-benchmarks/

UCAS (2022) *UCAS Freshers Report: Student Spends and Trends 2022*: https://www.ucas.com/file/583581/download?token=4DSTA9Vj

Films and videos

The Social Network – a film about the founders of the social networking website Facebook: www.imdb.com/title/tt1285016/

Simon Sinek, *Start with Why*: https://www.ted.com/talks/simon_sinek_ how_great_leaders_inspire_action

Regulatory guidance

Advertising Standards Authority (ASA) website: www.asa.org.uk/

ASA (2023) *Influencers' Guide to Making Clear That Ads Are Ads*: www.asa.org.uk/resource/influencers-guide.html

Facebook terms and policies: https://www.facebook.com/policies_ center/pages_groups_events/

General Data Protection Regulation (GDPR): www.ico.org.uk/for-organisations/guide-to-data-protection/guide-to-the-general-data-protection-regulation-gdpr/

Instagram promotion guidelines: https://help.instagram. com/179379842258600

Twitter guidelines for promotions: https://help.twitter.com/en/rules-and-policies/twitter-contest-rules

UK competition guidelines: https://www.asa.org.uk/advice-online/promotional-marketing-prize-draws-in-social-media.html

Training courses

Google: https://skillshop.withgoogle.com

Meta Blueprint: https://www.facebookblueprint.com/

LinkedIn Marketing Labs: https://training.marketing.linkedin.com/

TikTok Academy: https://my.academywithtiktok.com/learn

Useful tools and websites

Alt Text writing: www.alttext.ai

Awareness days: www.daysoftheyear.com, www.Onthisday.com, www.Thisdayinmusic.com

Broken link checker: https://ahrefs.com/broken-link-checker

Colour contrast analyser: https://color.adobe.com/create/color-contrast-analyzer

Emojis: www.emojipedia.com

Exploding Topics: https://www.explodingtopics.com

Fanpage Karma (social media analytics): www.fanpagekarma.com

Feedly (RSS reader): www.feedly.com

Google Alerts: www.google.com/alerts

Google Trends: https://trends.google.com

Hashtag research: hashtags.org, hashtagify.me, best-hashtags.com or the app Tagomatic

Image sizes: www.sproutsocial.com/insights/social-media-image-sizes-guide/

Influencer marketing: www.influencermarketinghub.com

Meta Ads Library: https://www.facebook.com/ads/library

Project management tools: www.asana.com, www.trello.com, www.monday.com

Social media management tools: Hootsuite (www.hootsuite.com), Sprout Social (www.sproutsocial.com), Tweetdeck (www.tweetdeck.com)

Social media monitoring tools: Brandwatch (www.brandwatch.com), Mentionlytics (www.mentionlytics.com), Talkwalker (www.talkwalker.com)

Social media news and resources library: www.thelighthouse.social

Semrush: https://www.semrush.com/social-media/

Semrush Social Tracker User Guide: https://www.semrush.com/kb/33-social-media-tool

TikTok Ads Library: https://ads.tiktok.com/business/creativecenter

Twitter Lists: https://help.twitter.com/en/using-twitter/twitter-lists

Video specifications: www.sproutsocial.com/insights/social-media-video-specs-guide/

Website performance testing: https://gtmetrix.com

Acknowledgements

Writing this book has been a collaborative effort, and I am deeply grateful to everyone who has supported me on this journey. Here are just a few of the incredible individuals who played a role in the creation of this book:

Laura, thank you for consistently challenging me with academic rigour. The process of research, preparation and analysis was truly an enjoyable experience. The biggest challenge of recording LinkedIn Lives with you is to remember that others are watching!

To all those who participated in the research studies in 2020 and 2022, thank you. Your contributions have been crucial: you have provided valuable insights and data that influenced the content of this book, and my work.

Kashyap Vyas, thank you for your skill and patience in creating figures based on the research data.

To my team of *Relax!* book reviewers, including Alanah, Beth, Elizabeth, Fiona, Helen, Jenny, Jerome, Louise, Lydia, Natasha, Paul, Rebecca, Roger, Sarah, Sarah, Shevy, Suzanne, Theresa, Tim and Tom. Thank you! Your comments and suggestions were immensely valuable. And to reviewers of this book, including Anna, Beth, Claire, Fran, Jake, Jonathan, Leigh, Lizzie, René, Tom and Tinisha. I appreciate the time and effort you all spent in providing feedback.

Andy, our update webinars are a highlight of every month. I love our geek-out sessions on the latest data and new features, and it's amazing to see how our discussions resonate with others. Thank you for providing the ContentCal case study.

Thanks also to Aimee, Darren, Helen, Joe, Michelle, Penny and Ross for sharing case studies and quotes.

Kim, thank you for your ongoing support, encouragement and feedback. This journey has been longer and more challenging than writing my first book, and your support has been invaluable. I hope the next book is a little easier!

René, I am incredibly grateful for your candid advice, and especially for making me realise that 'this is a completely different book' (not just a second edition).

Jenny, thank you for all the catch-ups and sense-checking.

Jane Hammett, your attention to detail during the editing process was exceptional. It was great to work with you again.

Jen, thank you for your dedication to keeping my website in shape, and for creating the tools to support the book. Rich, thanks for maintaining The Lighthouse as a valuable resource for social media marketers.

Elite Authors, thank you for your expertise in typesetting the print and e-book editions.

Justin Hill (The Other Operation), thank you for the enjoyable recording sessions and for bringing the audiobook to life.

To my best friend and husband, Steven. For your unwavering patience through the roller coaster of self-doubt and moments of accomplishment. I could not do what I do without you by my side.

Taylor – thanks for the chats!

Finally, to you, the reader – thank you for taking the time to read this book.

About the author

Luan Wise is a chartered marketer and fellow of the Chartered Institute of Marketing (FCIM) with more than 25 years of experience in agency, client-side and consultancy roles. She has worked across a variety of industry sectors, including postal services, manufacturing, recruitment, higher education and professional services – for household names, award-winning institutions, and smaller – but perfectly formed – local businesses.

Luan's career in marketing started 'web first', managing content and building online communities. She helped many organisations to produce their first websites. For most of her agency-side career, Luan worked for Hilton, planning and managing complex multimedia, multi-site promotional campaigns for its national and international chain of health clubs. In 2007 Luan switched to become a client-side marketer, joining a start-up business operating in the newly liberalised postal marketplace. With Luan's support, the business's annual sales fast-tracked from £3 million to £60 million within five years.

Seeking a new career challenge, in 2011 Luan started her own marketing consultancy and training business. Since then, she has provided project-based and ongoing support to organisations across the world. She has also delivered numerous industry event talks, group training to thousands of business professionals, plus guest lectures at university business schools.

Luan's expertise in social media was first recognised by LinkedIn as part of its International Women's Day #bestconnected campaign in 2015, which named her one of the top 5 female marketers in the UK. A year later she was signed as a course instructor for LinkedIn's online learning platform. Luan is also an accredited lead trainer for Meta (Facebook and Instagram) and a coach for Google's Digital Garage initiative.

Luan's response to the Covid crisis was to swap her car for a T5 campervan. She now enjoys travelling the UK as much as possible, documenting her #vanlife on TikTok.

Printed in Great Britain
by Amazon

32358856R00145